Monica Quarles

# A TRUE

Living with a Rare Disease

# MIRACLE

# A TRUE MIRACLE
### Living with a Rare Disease

Published by Krystal Lee Enterprises (KLE Publishing)
Copyright © 2025 by Monica Quarles All rights reserved.
Please send comments and questions:

Krystal Lee Enterprises
770-240-0089 Ext. 1
sales@KLEPub.com

To Reach the Author:
Email: monica@klepub.com

Web: www.monicaquarles.com
Facebook: AuthorMonicaQuarles

Printed in the United States of America.
All rights reserved. No part of this book may be reproduced or transmitted in any form or by any means, electronic or mechanical, including photocopying, recording, or any information storage and retrieval system without written permission of the publisher except for brief quotations used in reviews, written specifically for inclusion in a newspaper, blog, magazine, or academic paper.

ISBN: 978-1-945066-88-7

# DEDICATION

I dedicate this book to my husband, my children, family, and friends. Also, those who are caregivers and living with a rare diseases, this book is to inspire you.

Miracle, this is a gift for you. This book is to honor your life and share how grateful I am to be your mother and for all of your family who love you.

Thank you to my village, and those who are a village to families during their time of need. And a special thanks to my best friend Alicia, for always being in my corner and supporting me. I love you!

# A TRUE MIRACLE

Living with a Rare Disease

## Table of Contents

| | |
|---|---|
| Intro | 8 |
| Early Years | 12 |
| Mr. Right | 24 |
| Starting a Family | 40 |
| IVF Journey | 56 |
| Birth Story | 70 |
| Miracle Arrives Home | 80 |
| PPD | 88 |
| What Can Fall Down | 106 |
| God Shows Up | 124 |
| Liver | 140 |
| Closing | 156 |

*Monica Quarles*

# INTRO

This book is dedicated to anyone living with or caring for someone with a rare disease. The purpose of this book is to provide hope, share my personal story, create a safe space to navigate the challenges, and recognize that living with a rare disease is a true miracle and demonstrates God's beauty and wonder. I want to thank God for blessing me with my true miracle.

I thank God for my husband, children, and my village. I thank God for the beautiful people who have stood beside me when it felt like our lives were spiraling out of control. I had to learn through this journey that I am not alone, and that there are other people out there who are going through the same thing. I wanted to give everyone an opportunity to have a voice, especially those making a difference and others who share in the journey of living with a rare disease. I've learned in my journey that God has given you family, both natural and divine.

I've learned that family isn't defined by the people who share the same blood type, but rather by those who share the same heart posture. I thank God for the people He has placed in our lives, who have shown relentless love, kindness, and sacrifice, and have shared in both the joys and pains of our journey.

I learned through this journey that my village was composed of many different people outside of our natural family, including neighbors, friends, strangers, therapists, nurses, doctors, childcare providers, and supervisors. We truly have seen God through the hands and feet of these people, and we are forever grateful. I learned that you find help in the most unlikely places, and it's been utterly breathtaking.

It is my prayer that this book will truly help people realize that there is hope. There is joy. There are tears of both happiness and sorrow on this road, but it's worth it when you see your loved one smile and defy the odds stacked against them. This book is a piece of encouragement to remind you that what you are fighting for in your day-to-day life is worth it, or will be a True Miracle. My heart is that we connect and draw strength from each other's stories, and witness miracles.

*Monica Quarles*

# EARLY YEARS

I guess this is the part of the book where it's all about me and I talk about my back story. So you probably want to know about my parents, siblings, childhood friends, and begin with my birthday.

I was born on June 15th, 1984, on a summer Friday morning at 3:17am. I was 4 pounds. I was told I had a head full of hair because that's all my birth mother saw before giving me away for adoption. I was a premature baby; my birth mother shared that she remembers that day vividly. I know that my greatest fight has been with my family from birth. I came into this world in a fight.

I was conceived in the projects on the eastside of Indianapolis, where my mother was fighting for her life at the hands of my father. Faced with a choice to end the cycle of domestic violence and cut off ties with a troubled relationship, she made the decision that would affect her life and mine forever. My birth mother decided to place me for adoption, so I grew up in the system, not knowing my identity and roots. There was pain at the center of what *family* meant for me with my experiences of being displaced in foster care, group homes, and at one point, homeless etc. I was so desperate for love and looking in all the wrong places.

My adopted mother shared that I was abused in

foster homes and returned a few times because I cried a lot. I was about 15 months old when I went to live in a two-parent Christian home with my adopted parents. I grew up with an older brother who was funny and, for the most part, nice to me. I guess we were still siblings and went through what all kids go through. I remember always wanting to be close to him and do whatever he did. We watched and played wrestling. We loved "The Undertaker." But when his friends were around, I was no longer cool. That really sucked. He was all I had and my dog Spike.

As a family, we spent a lot of time together. We would go on vacations and spend a lot of time at the beach. Most of the people in my adopted family were all musically gifted. I remember going to church on a regular basis. I felt like one of the family, and it didn't dawn on me that I was adopted for many years.

My older brother was only four years older than I, so we were connected. We fought and argued over stuff like toys and the things we wanted. It was in one of those petty arguments that he said, "That's why you are adopted." At first, I thought it was a joke, but after reading his face, I knew he said something that he wished he hadn't.

I wasn't familiar with the term, so when he said it, I replied with an attitude, "I am glad to be adopted." I don't know why I didn't think to ask my parents about what it meant. I remember going to my teacher and asking about it. In school, I was the chatterbox when growing up. I enjoyed school, having friends, and I was the life of the party. All the children would come to my parties and events. I guess in my own way, I was popular.

My teacher told me, "I don't want to give you the

definition, but it means that your parents are not your birth parents." I was floored. I had no idea that I was adopted. I can't say it didn't change anything because it did. I started to look at everything that was off in the relationship and wondered if it was off because I was adopted.

I am not sure when I started to struggle with my self-worth, but looking back as an adult, I could see the writing on the wall. As I battled my internal questions of who my parents are? Why did they leave me? And would they ever want me back? I soul-searched and longed for the mother I didn't know. I was close to my adopted father, but something in me didn't connect as closely with my adopted mother.

As a mother, I think I know what it is. We all know we were born and connected to a woman who carried us for nine months. Who decided to deliver us and not abort us, even though she could have for any circumstance? She loved me enough to make sure I got here, and for that, I will always love her and respect her decision to choose life. The feeling of connection with my birth mother increased when I was 9, 10, 11, and 12 years old. I longed for her in ways one could only imagine.

I think every adopted child wonders if their birth parents will come for them or look for them at some point. I had hoped that she would. I think what also made the bond difficult for me and my adopted mother was that she showed her affection differently than I had hoped. I wanted to hear "I love you" and get cute nicknames from her. She wasn't a lovey-dovey like my father was. He gave me nicknames like "Pumpkin" and "Junebug," and always told me he loved me.

Having parents who are expressive and say how

much they love you each day does impact how a child feels and if they "know" they are loved. When I had children, I made sure to tell them I loved them every day if not more than once. I gave them hugs like my father gave me and I hardly spanked my children, because my dad made that a last resort.

My adopted mother was more of the strong arm in the family, and she seemed to hand out more beatings than I ever wanted to give to my children. I know some parenting styles are different and rooted in different rules. A lot of "old school" parents probably thought whippings were the best form of discipline, but I agreed more with my father that they weren't.

It felt so cold to get disciplined physically by her because we weren't that close to begin with. She didn't have expected rules like belts; she would use her hands and switches, braided up branches from the tree, to discipline. So if she didn't like something I did or said, it would be her hand slapping me in the back of the head, in the mouth, or hitting me in the chest. It was awkward to say the least, and I knew when I endured it I didn't want to treat my children that way.

I have always been an outgoing, full-of-life personality, but I was also raised to be respectful. I wouldn't openly disrespect or be disobedient. I had to be sneaky or do things secretly because I feared my parents and God. Growing up in the church, you were told that God was watching your every move. I felt like God was the one you didn't want to cross or make angry, so you do your best not to make him mad. I really had a deep-seated fear of God growing up.

Even when I did bad things, I was waiting to be

struck down or instantly rebuked. I guess I kinda found out how he could be merciful because he didn't. I wanted to be like him, in that I wanted people to love me and respect me, not just be afraid of me. I had two best friends, Sharee and Alicia, growing up who I knew loved me like sisters.

We were all three close, and my mom and there's sensed trouble, I guess with us all hanging out together for long periods or unsupervised. I could never spend the night over their houses when I asked. I think in all the years that I had known them, I attended 3 slumber parties because my parents were so strict.

So, yeah, growing up, I was kind of a sheltered, outgoing person. I didn't get to go to school parties, dances, or anything that looked like the devil could show up. My parents had a very tight leash on my whereabouts. Now, I took some notes to ensure my children were safe, but I had to learn how to let them breathe, that wasn't them breathing. That wasn't an easy task unfortunately ,because we tend to repeat what was rehearsed.

I went to a traditional school through elementary and middle school. Funny how you can still find trouble even when you are not invited to the gatherings. I remember getting in trouble mostly for talking in school. The girls I loved to hang out with we started getting into trouble in middle school, so the IPS and township schools I was zoned for changed. When I went to high school, I was enrolled in a Christian school.

I felt like removing me from my friend was torture. It felt like God was punishing me for being a kid, and my parents were the ones who made sure that I was miserable. Everything felt like it was about God, but only about

God. There was no room for mistakes, fun, or being a kid with problems. I had to be perfect, and I hated it. I wanted to be normal, and maybe that's why I wanted my mother. I am sure she had flaws like I did, and I want to relate to someone.

I went through a season of rebellion when I was ripped away from my friends. I hated chapel because I felt like none of my prayers were being heard. I felt out of place sometimes because this wasn't the life I picked, but the one I was forced into. I was grateful, yes, but I still wanted to know where I got my mouth and personality from. I didn't see it in my adopted parents, so maybe that's why they didn't know how to help me rule it as good.

I wanted to figure it out, and without the support I needed, I turned to love in other places to find myself. I thought I knew what to do. I can see how I was wrong, and my rebellion made my life harder. I didn't finish school, I dropped out, and the boyfriend I had in high school helped me to become a teen mom.

I knew I was a wild child, and my parents seemed not to want to deal with my rebellion, and I couldn't blame them, although I wanted them to show they loved me. They sent me away to finish my pregnancy, and it was when I felt dumped, not just by the boyfriend, but by my family, that I was determined to give the life I didn't have to my son. I determined in my heart to be something and to have something for myself, but especially for him.

I refused to allow my feelings of being hopeless and discarded to control how I would see myself. It did hurt like I was in hell, to feel them turn their backs on me. It was like, "Nope, Monica. You have done it now. You have reached your final lifeline, and we cannot help you." Getting pregnant felt like the last straw.

The lesson you would have thought I learned from being adopted, I actually learned from being abandoned. When I was cast aside and put under a lampshade by my family, I was embraced by strangers. They were the ones who reminded me that I had value and the baby I was carrying. They didn't remind me of my sins and wrong deeds; they pointed to the future and what God could and wanted to do for me.

I remember thinking, like, "Dang, Jesus. This is so cold. When I mess up, are you gonna just throw me away like this?" He answered me through strangers. The relationships I built here changed my story and trajectory for my life. God will give you a village that might not share your home, but can understand or empathize with your journey. This was the first lesson I applied later in life when I had to deal with a challenge for my Miracle.

I remember this woman, Luann, who latched on to me as soon as I got to the maternity home. She told me to my face, "I'm gonna love you anyway. Give me a hug. I'm not scared of your attitude." I didn't ask her to love me or connect with me; she did it out of her own heart. Words cannot express how much she impacted me.

What was most important, she meant it. She loved me. I saw that in her eyes, and she cared about me as my pregnancy progressed. She got me to think of life differently. I started to ask and think, what can I do differently? I couldn't change my parents, but I could work on changing myself.

I remember thinking, "I couldn't change my mom

giving me up for adoption. I couldn't change my adopted mom and adopted dad sending me away. I couldn't change how I used to feel about it, but I could change how I was gonna feel. I could change myself for my son and be the best that I could be. This thinking started a new spark in my life."

This spark gave me the drive to want to work. I started working while I was pregnant and saving money for the things I needed for our apartment. I wanted a car for us to get around, and help us to be independent. I knew then that I wanted to return to school, finish college, and get married someday.

I wanted to marry the man who I had my son with. I thought we would become a family and share the responsibility of raising our child together. I didn't know my birth family at the time, but I realized my adopted parents weren't making any attempt to get back into my life. They were done with me–at least for the time being. I refused to think of giving my son up for adoption, I was determined to stay and figure this thing out.

I feel like my adopted mom wore the pants in the relationship so even if my dad wanted to be there for me, she could heavily influence if he was or wasn't. My dad was this kinda laid back guy, and he went with the flow. My dad loved his music and hosting parties. He was entertaining, somebody who can make you feel at home. I don't recall him and my mom ever being lovey dovey, just good partners.

They worked well with ministry, too. They would hold bible study at our house and the two of them would sing together and teach. They appeared to be on one front although they didn't agree on everything. My mom would say no when my dad would say yes. They would talk and often it was a no afterward.

I liked that they figured it out even if it wasn't perfect. They made me want to get married to have that also. I remember dreaming of a Cinderella wedding and experience with the big gown and everything. I wanted the fanfare, the beauty, and elegance of it all.

I knew marriage was work looking at the two of them, though. I get that you have to have both parts to make a balanced family. If we always heard yes like my dad said, and not enough no, the pendulum would swing in the other direction. I don't hate my upbringing because there was a lot of good, I just look for the ways I could make things better for my children.

On the flipside, I always felt like I was the black Cinderella for many reasons. I had this stepmother who reminded me sometimes of the evil stepmother with her discipline. Sometimes cleaning up and not feeling wanted, made you just feel like a worker and not family. I had a brother and not two sisters, which was a good thing. One brother who could say something cruel was enough.

I know he meant it at the time but wasn't expecting it to hurt me as much as it did; but I do see the resemblance of her story and mine. I used to say to myself, one day, Mr. Right is gonna come and find me. He will fall madly in love with me, he will whisk me off to get married, and I'm gonna be out of here. My life would be amazing and I would get "a happily ever after." I've always been a person that loves stories and romance and things like that for as long as I can remember.

So, yeah, that was my early years.

*Monica Quarles*

*Monica Quarles*

# MR. RIGHT

Okay, so finding Mr. Right wasn't the ideal road. I didn't totally wait around for him. I was a little busy and kissed a couple of frogs before he found me, but he got to me at the right time. Sometimes your plans don't go as planned, and you have to learn to work with it and pull through.

Funny, my husband told me before I even started this book, those other relationships didn't count, so I will say that my Mr. Right came after despair, heartbreak, and divorce. I had been divorced for some time and didn't plan on doing it again. I was disappointed and embarrassed to have failed. I felt the judgment of others who thought the worst because I could not keep my marriage together, and I allowed that to bother me.

When I failed to keep things together with my son's father, I was determined to make the next one work. I wanted to have the whole thing: family, marriage, a good job, and for life to be good. When I got divorced, it tore all of that up. I didn't have this cute situation that made me feel better about my life. I was left with tattered ends and another failed relationship that left me in a dark place.

I felt really ashamed. I walked in shame, because I just felt like they were right about me. I was a screw up and maybe I didn't deserve love; maybe I was unlovable. I started thinking this was why I kept being alone or tossed to the side. I know I was on the deep end, but I was broken. And sometimes we want the right thing, but at the wrong time, and we're not quite ready for what we think we're ready for.

I think for me, being young and a single mom, I didn't wanna be a single mom who was shunned in the church. I wanted to redeem my name and clean up my act. I wanted to be something that was pleasing to God. I knew shacking up was wrong and I needed to get married to have more children.

I felt judged for having a child out of wedlock, and I wanted the storm cloud to come from above my head. So when I started to engage in marriage interactions, like sex, I knew I had to get married. I would hear people say, "It's better to marry than burn." So I jumped into marriages like people date. The men weren't good to me, and if I am honest, I should have demanded more of them.

They weren't healthy for me. They were not faithful, and they didn't value me like I knew I should have been. I wasn't sure at first if it was the men or me. I thought maybe I deserved what I was going through, and this is what marriage was about. But the more I stayed, the harder and more depressed I became.

I got to a low place, so low that I didn't want marriage or anybody anymore. I wanted to be alone, where I was free, even if I was lonely. These skewed versions of marriage were an early example of my skewed version of family. I didn't expect them to stay, if I was honest. I didn't expect them to be good, loving, and kind. I was too tolerant of too much, hoping to earn what I should have always deserved.

I was disappointed with the relationship, and even the proposals left me wanting more. I cannot say they persuade me intensely to want to marry them, more than my ideal of marriage encouraged me to say "yes." I felt so much pain while being married, and then I felt trapped to have to stay in it. When you are weak, you can do things you don't want to do because you feel you have no other choice. I didn't want God to look down on me, and I wanted to be married to a good partner. I just didn't know how to achieve it.

If I am honest, a factor in my choice to get married prematurely was that I wanted to have good sex. I wanted to, you know, have this ideal picket fence looking world where I could live my happily ever after. But there was a lot of work to be done. There was a lot of work that wasn't done in me. I can't blame my exes for everything that I allowed; I had to see the fault in me also, but most importantly, I had to see what was causing me pain.

I had to learn to take ownership of my part in why my relationships failed, too, and acknowledge my brokenness. Sometimes we want our broken pieces to be healed by someone else, but that is God's business. Like, he is our healer, and healing is his business. I needed him to heal me, not a man, not a marriage, not things, but God, I came to realize.

So I had to learn that lesson. But what I will say is, God healing me didn't mean I had to marry again. I could have forfeited everything I loved about marriage, and God would have been enough for me. After the disappointment and pain I experienced, I didn't care to deal with that again. I can understand how so many give up after a few failed marriages or bad relationships because I was there too.

What I learned, when we stop caring about finding Mr. Right, that is when he shows up. He comes when we are complete in ourselves and healed, ideally by God, so that we can receive him. I wanna say that the right moment in my life and growth was when my Mr. Right came, my husband.

When I met him through work, he was actually going through a hard time in his life and going through a divorce as well. I think that we just met each other at the right time, honestly. The funny thing about it is that we had already crossed each other's paths and didn't even know it. I was actually cool with his cousin, and grew up with his cousin in church. It was just so funny to see how things work out like that in life sometimes.

I remember telling her, "I met this guy who looks exactly like you. You could be brother and sister, ya'll look so much alike." I got to talking some more and showing pictures, and she said, "Girl, that's my cousin." When I met him, I wasn't thinking about marriage or anything. I just wanted to be there for him and be a friend.

But something about him wouldn't let me friend-zone him. I wasn't sure if it was his smile. How he talked to me, or just the character he had that drew me closer to him. I guess it was all of it because I kept thinking about him more and more. He had something about him that was warm and inviting. He actually reminded me of someone who I loved a lot, my adopted father.

When we would talk and I would catch him looking at me, he gave me this warm and loving feel like how my dad did growing up. I felt like he really saw me. I could tell that he loved me when he saw me, and that he liked everything about me. Sometimes you can meet the right one, and they just make you feel desired, loved, wanted, and you can't get away even if you tried. I might not have had any plans, but he clearly had plans for me.

When he determined I was the woman for him, it was no faking it. You know, when someone is pretending and trying hard to convince you of what you already know is wasting your time. I could speed past all of that. But when the right one comes, all the stuff you said about being single forever, just like that, would be gone. When I looked at him, I was like, wow, I love this man. There is something different about him, I don't know what it is, but I love it.

You ever felt like that before? Maybe it's just me who was on the job trying to help someone who came to my office, and at a time where I am doing my social work, I am over here getting invested. I never made my business personal, never crossed that line. I am a professional, and it has always been that way for me. But something about him made me care about his children, his livelihood, and wellbeing.

Like I said, I did this everyday but I never got involved. So, day by day, I felt myself wanting to be there and help him with his children during his hardship. What was crazy about all of this, while I was helping him, I was going through a similar situation in my own life. Isn't it like God to call you to help someone else while you too are getting help, too?

I was like, it's funny that God will pull you from a place where you feel like you're lacking and say, "No. We are not going to think like that, Monica. Let's not think about you. Let's think about somebody else." So, I stopped worrying about me and my problems and started caring more for others. I always think that's kinda funny how that works out.

After meeting him things took a natural progression. I remember our first date at Top Golf. It was light and the feeling he gave me felt like soft pink butterflies in my heart. I was floating on cloud nine as we hung out and laughed. I love to laugh, and he brought that side out on the date. But what took me back the most, was how he saw the queen in me, too.

Some men can help you to have fun, but they treat you like a friend or a homie. He didn't do that. He got us massages before we went golfing to end the date, and I was in heaven, feeling relaxed and refreshed. There is a way to love a woman without sex, and I liked how we explored that. He made me feel valuable and important. He reminded me with the little things that I was royalty. He catered to a part in me I had long forgotten and was overlooked before.

That first date was my first date and experience with a man who I believe genuinely wanted to know and love me without strings or hidden agendas. It was the first time I felt like this in my life. He was a perfect gentleman who knew how to pull out the little girl, who was giddy and longing for romance, to the surface.

He held my hand when we walked together. He would give me the side eye grin that just made me melt on the inside. I couldn't let him know how well he was doing at first, but when he opened the door for me, pulled out my chair, and let me order first–I was with it.

# Mr. Right

I could trust a man like this to guide me, you know? But I ain't gonna lie, at the end of the night he did try to get a kiss, and although I loved everything he did, I didn't give him a kiss. He was working, but he had to work a bit harder to get a kiss from me.

I knew that was the test. If he wanted me, for real, he would work for me. He would respect who I am and show up for me because it is in him. I had to make sure he wasn't a one-trick pony. I kissed a frog before, and I wasn't doing that again. But this date was magical; it felt unlike anything I had experienced. I didn't want this moment to die or end. I could have stayed out all night if I didn't have things to do the next day, and it could be appropriate, you know?

The whole date was just perfect and light. That margarita pizza we had was perfect like all the other details. I couldn't wait to see him again. I gotta tell you, I was apprehensive about him driving me and picking me up, because I didn't know him that well yet, so I drove. Ending the date in the parking lot of Top Golf was good for us. I would tell any woman to set boundaries for yourself. If you want to be married, value yourself and don't let anyone cheapen that, ever. They will work for you, and if not, move on and stand alone if you have to. Mr. Right will come.

I remember as we were getting to know each other, I told him I was moving away. He said, "You can't move away." I replied, "And why not?" Then he said, "You can't move anywhere because you are supposed to be here. I know you don't wanna hear this, but you are supposed to be my wife."

I would giggle and say, "You know I don't want to

hear that." I was seriously tired of hearing that, though. I got proposals and got married before. I didn't want to become another forgotten part in someone's life. I didn't want to lose myself again after spending so much time trying to find myself. Hearing the words ripped a part of my heart for a bit, and it stung. I refused to fail again, and the sad part, I almost refused to love again.

When you have married a man who didn't know how to be a husband to you in a God kind of way, you can run away from marriage. I almost ran away from my husband because I was scared of a repeat of my past. I felt it was all too much. I wanted to get out of this state because I was in a lot of pain here. I had a momma who didn't want me here. Adopted parents who didn't want me here, and my son's father, who didn't want me here. I didn't want to add anything else.

After my divorce, I had to add that on too. I felt like nobody in this state could want me, and I needed to have a clean slate somewhere else, you know? But that's when Robert melted my heart and said, "But I want you. I don't want you to leave me." I had heard this before, though. My ex told me he wanted me too, and look at what happened to that, I thought for a second.

Then I remember Robert looking me in my eyes and calming my spirit as he said, "I want you to be here with me." My heart wanted to be there with him, but my mind, or my instincts, told me to run. I couldn't stay, and I was restless. I ended up moving to Seattle to see if that was gonna be my home. I kid you not, that man got on the plane and came all the way from Indiana to Seattle to tell me, "This is not your home. Your home is back in Indiana with me. You're not supposed to be here, but I will be here, because you are supposed to be with me."

# Mr. Right

My trip to Seattle was brief. I never had someone to love me like I loved them. I would have done anything for my son, and this man had that kind of commitment to me to leave everything back home, to come and see about me. I remember telling him, "I don't have any family in Indiana." He kindly said, "That's where you are wrong, because you have me. I am your family now."

My heart was trying to give in, but the devil was taunting me. He reminded me of all the relationships that I had tried, that failed. I was afraid, embarrassed, and my mind kept running. I think Robert saw the fear that tried to replace what he was trying to do. I left Indiana in March, and by June of that same year, he said, "I came here to bring you home."

I was ready to leave Seattle and move back, but I wasn't sure about us and marriage. I was a runner, so anything could be enough for me to question what we were really doing. I looked at logical things like where we would live and how we would come together as a family. He lived in a small house on the Far East Side with his boys.

I had a daughter who was still young enough to live with me. I would ask him, "How would that work?" He said, "Easy, I will just build her a room." It sounded so easy, but I still wasn't sure. I couldn't fail again, and so I needed to have someone whom I trusted to help me make this decision. By this time, he was asking me to marry him, but I had to be sure.

Although my father and I had not been close in several years, we still talked every once in a while. I remember calling him and asking him what he thought about everything. "Dad, I met this really nice guy. He has three boys living with him, and I have my son and my daughter. I couldn't have my daughter sharing a room with all the boys in a two-bedroom house. So he told me he was gonna make her a room."

My Dad heard me talk and then he said calmly, "That's the one, honey. That's the one you should marry. If he makes a room for you in a little old house, you live in that house with that man because that means that he is making provision for you. And he will, you know, he will do what needs to be done to take care of his family and take care of his woman."

I thought that this was crazy. My dad never told me to marry anybody I had mentioned to him before, not even my ex-husband. This was gonna be a different life for us because we were in the suburbs on the other side of town. He had a two bedroom house but he was willing to do for me what no one else thought to do. He got on a plane, he has never rode in a plane a day in his life, but he did it twice.

When he came back the second time, he helped me pack and ship my things, then he drove me 32 hours to get us back to Indiana, and I knew this man was serious. With his actions he anchored my heart in the love and confidence he had for our family. When I couldn't see it, he saw it for us. When I asked, "Where is home?" He kept reminding me that home was with him and what we could build together.

And I think about that now. And, we were just so different, but I like that about us. In the beginning he taught me about some things that I knew nothing about. I didn't know much about the world, other than how what I tried to do didn't work and was very unfulfilling. It got me in a lot of trouble and a lot of heartache and pain.

He was so sweet to help me drive and we had fun on the trip laughing and talking through all the states. You know if you can survive a road trip with somebody for that long, you could figure anything else out. On that trip we started to build our world together in that short amount of time. I remember us singing and worshiping God together as we drove because God has always been at the center of our relationship. It was just pure bliss.

Our children met and everybody just really got along well. We dated for about two years, from 2018 to 2020 when we got married. Our blended family had three children from him and two from my side. It was perfect and I wouldn't change a thing, even us getting married during COVID.

My dream of having a fairytale wedding was drastically changing because of COVID. I remember the venue telling us, "Hey. You have to pay this money, no matter if one person comes or nobody comes." We were like dang. Oh my goodness." We were afraid that many people wouldn't come, so we eloped and still saved our date to have my fairytale wedding on our terms.

We got married on June 15th, 2020 on my birthday, but did the ceremony on August 8 that same year. I had my Cinderella Wedding. God is so faithful, people are still talking about how glamorous our wedding was when we held the celebration later that year. When we did have the ceremony, we weren't worried about who would come. It was about us, and that's how we kept it. We both had been married before, so all the fanfare with people wasn't as big of a deal.

I remember us being so moved at both ceremonies

that we cried. I cried so much on my birthday because this was a day that reminded me of so much pain, and for that pain to be replaced by the love I felt on that day was beyond words. We needed these events for us, we both had pain and challenges we learned to overcome together, and our ceremonies were a testament of the work we put into our marriage before anything was signed. We both believed in it.

I thought it might be selfish to share my birthday with my wedding anniversary on one hand, but I saw it as the best gift on the other. With COVID shutting down the world, the first day we could say yes, was the day we did it and that was June 15th on my birthday. It was so beautiful and I will never forget it.

Although June 15th was our day, the day we actually celebrate with our family and friends is in August. This ceremony was out of the Cinderella movie for real. My adopted dad married us, both of my moms were there (birth mom and adopted mom), and everything just felt magical. I got the horse ride caddy with the peek-a-boo window on the door. We got plenty of pictures of me and my husband in our white. We were smiling, and beyond happy the whole day. We were so glamorous, making me feel like the black Cinderella.

Because of COVID, our trip to Hawaii was canceled, but we ended up going to a fun park instead. We went to Cedar Point and had a great time. No matter where Robert and I may be, we know how to bring the fun; and it just so happens, I love amusement parks. I had the best wedding I could have ever asked for with the right prince this time, which made this wedding 10,000 times more wonderful than I could have ever imagined.

# Mr. Right

We had the time of our lives and it was so fun. We ate well, laughed, joked, and acted like we were big kids falling in love with each other. We really know how to have fun together by joking around, watching movies, and listening to music. Life can be simple when you are truly in love, the God kind of way.

What made this marriage also different was the kind of support we had. Between the two of us, we invested in each other's dreams. We built business together, pursued our careers, and we made good money together as a team. This was what I wanted all my life, to be a partner and not feel like I was in a marriage by myself.

Our marriage was really good and thriving. We were in love, happy, and we thought to share that love with our children. This love is what made room for Miracle. She was born to a couple who wanted her. She had siblings and a number of people who couldn't wait to meet her as soon as they all found out about her. We all wanted to grow and expand our family.

*Monica Quarles*

*Monica Quarles*

# STARTING A FAMILY

My life hasn't always been filled with the kind of love I have now. In my marriage, I feel safe, wanted, and free. In my previous pregnancies from my relationships prior to my current marriage, my life was different. Being 17 years old and becoming a mother for the first time, my thoughts were also very different.

I was the type of mother who thought I looked good pregnant. I embraced my journey. I loved the changes in my stomach, and I felt just as sexy with my bump as I did without. My social life didn't slow down because I was pregnant either. I was still working, hanging with my friends, and doing what I wanted to do.

I didn't feel that I had to stay at home and just wait around for my baby to come. I was out doing things, walking, and enjoying my social life. Even in the group home, I eventually found a way to still live while being pregnant. No, I didn't know everything when I was 17 about how to be a good mother to my son–but I knew that was my goal.

Before he was born, I had intended to welcome a healthy baby boy into my life. He was born at a good time in my life, though many would have said I was too young. I don't think anyone can prepare enough to become a parent. Every child is different. Initially, I was scared when my son was first born.

A lot of changes were happening with my body and my mind as the months passed. I had a tough time adjusting to my family dynamics changing and trying to build with my son's father. I always knew my life would change drastically when our son was born. What I didn't know was that I would have to go it alone in the early years because my son's father was incarcerated during the later part of my pregnancy. He wasn't going to be a part of his life right away, so I had to get used to the idea of being a mother and taking on full responsibility. To work through this change, I had to focus on the positives.

It was hard, and I won't lie or sugarcoat my feelings. I never wanted to be a single mom, and do it all by myself, because I never had that example growing up. I was used to having two parents in the home. All of my parents' friends were married, so no one could relate to what I was going through at the time except other girls in the group home with me. When I had morning sickness and was going through the motions of pregnancy, it was nice to have people around to lean on.

I would try to eat certain things, and my son would be like, "Nope, can't eat that," you know? I tried to do everything I wanted to do as a teenager, but my son was strong. He would make me sick to my stomach and change my plans all the time.

I was grateful that morning sickness didn't last my entire pregnancy, but for a brief period. I was pretty happy after that phase passed. Even after my son was born, it didn't really hit me how hard my life would become because I saw him as a blessing.

## Starting a Family

At first, all I could think about was having a cute little baby to dress up and play with or whatever. I didn't think about those sleepless nights that would quickly follow. I always say, Chordae, he's the strongest, probably because he got a different version of a mother than what my other children had. I learned from my mistakes with him. I had to grow up because I chose to mother him and love him through my actions.

Chordae was a very active baby. He walked early and talked pretty much at about two years old. Chordae was born healthy, but he was a crier. He had colic, really bad, and struggled with gas. There were many times when I visited the hospital early on because I didn't know how to console him. I would feed him, burp him, and change his diaper, but nothing soothed his crying.

I would sit there and just cry with him because I didn't know what to do sometimes. I realized sometimes you just have to be there through the storm and do what you can to help. We worked through that process together, and we are both stronger for it. I never had a problem with feeding him or knowing what he wanted as he grew older. Him being my oldest, I would talk to him like I would talk to anyone else, and likely that's how he picked up vocabulary so quickly.

I knew we had to get our own place and space to get comfortable. The center stopped being the place I felt comfortable, and I desired more. I wanted more for my son and myself. I wanted my own apartment, and I knew I needed to get a car.

I also knew I needed a job to sustain anything for us. I had to work hard to take care of my son and pay the bills and stuff. The maternity home was in Saint Joe,

Mishawaka, away from my friends and family. I had to lean on the social workers and the new community I was building to get around the small town. I didn't know much about the area, so I had to learn on my own.

It was tough, and I knew when I got my own place, I wanted to be back around people I knew–even if the only thing familiar was the city. So I moved back with Chordae and got my own place. Soon after, I met a man who I thought would help me build the family I desired.

To say the least, Mr. Right did not come along for a long time after I ended up with another Mr. Wrong, hoping to find love and family in that relationship. I became pregnant with my daughter Monae. I remember thinking: *Oh my God, I'm trying to figure things out with my son, and now I will have a daughter, too.* I have more pressure on me to be an even better mom to her because she reminded me of some of the wounds I had as a little girl. I didn't want to pass them down to her.

I enjoyed shopping and dressing my little girl every day. I liked for my daughters to be girly, girls. I tried to give her all the things she needed, and my son, including love and compassion. Things didn't work out with me and her father; I found out quickly when she was born. I still had the dream of having a family, so I thought about trying to make things work with my son's father. He was waiting to pick up where we left off. But it also didn't work in the long run.

The pregnancy with my daughter was different than the first. I felt like I had morning sickness for months on end. To make things worse, my relationship wasn't stable. Getting pregnant again didn't make things work out with us but made my job twice as hard. I had to raise my son still alone with the rocky relationship with his father, and now, I faced raising my daughter and going through this pregnancy also with very little help. I was more scared than before, and for different reasons. I was like, you know, here I am again in the same situation. I really wanted to have a family, a marriage, a dog, and a picket white fence–but here I am back in the same predicament and worse off than before.

This double dose of rejection, abandonment, and infidelity stained my perception of relationships. In this marriage to my son's father, my desire for family within the scope of marriage was distorted and ripped apart. I wanted it so badly, but I didn't know how to obtain it. I just knew I loved my children dearly, and I wanted to be a better mom and person.

I shifted my focus from the traditional family construct to how I could be the best single mom I could be for my children. I acknowledged my good traits and worked on improving my bad ones. I didn't take my frustrations out on my children for the mistakes of their fathers. I was determined to live in the best neighborhood so that they could attend good schools. I knew I needed to do my part, and I was willing to work hard and go to school.

I won't say that there weren't any challenges to doing what I had to do; I was frustrated because it felt like I was being punished for being an unwed mother. You can see the eyes and feel the judgment. I just had to bury some of my pain by working hard. I attended school and was able to pursue a college education, ultimately becoming a CNA. I remember taking the kids to school with me while I was in college, as I earned my associate's degree in human resources, my bachelor's degree in social work, and ultimately my master's degree in business management. My children were a constant part of my journey, motivating me and keeping me focused.

I became a CNA young and that kept money coming in the house. I thank God for teaching me how to survive and navigate these years of my life. I had my own car so getting to the people who could help me wasn't a problem. Finding babysitters did become a problem when I wanted to go back to school.

I had to find daycare services that could accommodate my busy schedule and financial situation. I still didn't have the help of my adopted family or friends; they were busy living the lives they wanted and I couldn't blame them even though I could have used their help. I wasn't mad, but at times I did get sad because I didn't have the kind of support system I needed.

I used to think it was a punishment for the choices I made. Not sure if I was the only one who ever felt like that. I relied heavily on state and government programs to help me early on in my parenting journey and I think this is what created the hunger in me to help others. I benefited greatly from people being kind to me and I wanted to share that kindness with others.

I wished I could have been around more instead of working and being at school so much. I felt like I was missing so much of Chordae's life with working as much as I did. Carrying Monae in my stomach with this hectic schedule also didn't help me with balancing my diet. I got much bigger with her than I did with my son.

This time around, I didn't feel as pretty as I did when I was pregnant with Chordae. Of my three pregnancies,

Monae was my largest baby, weighing nine pounds and twelve ounces. I gave birth to her naturally, same as Chordae, who was seven pounds and three ounces. Miracle was six pounds and fourteen ounces, but I'm kinda getting ahead of myself right now.

Let's back up a bit. I remember being told girls make you sick to your stomach, so I knew she was a girl before my ultrasound. I think my self-esteem was definitely different when I was pregnant with my daughter. I think I overate because I wasn't happy about things in my life, and I struggled to find balance. I think the way a woman feels does impact how she goes through her pregnancy, and if I could share anything about it. I would encourage every woman to find a way to see her beauty even in the midst of a storm.

It was during this pregnancy that my stretch marks came and never went away. My body definitely changed after giving birth to Monae. And so, it took me a while to bounce back from that pregnancy, and I was fairly young at that time. This, too, added to my discomfort and growing self-esteem problem. Although I struggled with myself, I tried to keep it from impacting my children or allowing me to enjoy them. I never once regretted having my children–not even at my young age; they were the best thing that could have happened to me. They were so much fun and just so cute, they were mine and I was theirs. They loved me unconditionally.

It made my heart proud to give them their own rooms. It didn't seem like having their own rooms was always a good thing because it meant I had to clean up three rooms instead of two. It was like they would double team, junking one room and entering the other to do the same.

*Monica Quarles*

Whenever I would go to their rooms searching for them, I would find them lying underneath each other like puppies. They were two peas in a pod. I loved how close they were and enjoyed seeing them love one another like I longed to have with my siblings. Monae definitely had pieces of my personality; she had sass and pizzazz. She had an attitude from day one. Monae kept me laughing. She has always been funny, even with her attitude. We share a lot of laughs, even today; some things don't change. Chordae, I would say, had a heart like mine and was sensitive to other people's feelings. He is my gentle giant.

He is laid back, loves to laugh, and is pretty cool to be around, even now as an adult. If anything could be funny, he was the first to laugh and would outlast anyone in a laughing contest. They had different personalities, and still to this day, but they're both funny and act like they did as children.

My daughter has always been passionate and strong-willed. She is unforgettable, loud, and proud. My son is quiet and chill. He won't go there unless you push him after his patience has run out. I am like that, too, I guess. I have been patient for a long time, and as I grew older, I got even better at it. They were both really good kids, and as expected, in the teenage years, we had some rough patches, but we got through.

In the teenage years, I saw my oldest daughter use her hands to build things, do hair, nails, and be creative. Chordae is musically gifted and loves real estate. They both told me their plans for the future, and it is funny to see them living them now. My daughter said she wanted to live in Greenwood, and funny thing, she lives just outside of Greenwood today.

# Starting a Family

I'm pretty sure I put a lot of pressure on them because they were my everything. I wanted to make sure they succeeded and had a better step into life than I did, filled with support and confidence. I know I held them with a tight grip, but not too tight, by being super religious. I didn't want them to rebel, but to be respectable and responsible.

It was a battle, to say the least, but I was able to overcome and give them the best that I could. There was trouble for those two as teenagers for sure, and they got spankings when they were younger. I didn't wanna have to give spankings, but that was how I grew up. I wasn't brutal with any punishment I gave, like I experienced. But I was open to other ways of parenting.

When I found out that taking things away can also do the job, I started doing that too. There is no guidebook to parenting, so we all will have to learn as we grow. One thing I didn't want them to ever question was my love for them. I never wanted them to question if they were loved or wanted. I sat them down and told them about my life, the parts relevant, and how much I loved them often.

I wanted to push them to achieve their dreams and know that anything was possible, especially if they were willing to work for it. When I felt alone, it brought me so much comfort at this time, just knowing that I had My Babies     When my children began to have friends who became my honorary children, it made me feel good to give back like my adoptive parents did for me. I enjoyed my best friend's children becoming my God Children. I couldn't imagine how big my family would become over the years, but I am grateful.

I remembered being in my early 20's and deciding

that I wanted to find out who my birth mother and birth family were in hopes of creating this family for me and my children. I got to thinking of it only being the three of us, and how difficult it has already been. I was okay with being single, but to have no family also was a lot to accept. My children and I would need more than just me at some point in their lives. I found my biological family when I was about 23 years old, and I think that is when another part of my story changed. Now, I have the answers to my questions of who I came from and who my family was in my family lineage.

If you have been adopted and you feel like meeting your birth parents is something you need, no age is too late to try and find your family. Meeting them doesn't mean you are going to walk away holding hands. After we met them, they still felt like strangers to me. Give yourself time to catch up with the experience. Don't be quick to force yourself to embrace this part of your family if you are not ready, or may not feel it is time to introduce your children.

Something I noticed my children were struggling with, like me, was an absent parent. We were all going through an identity crisis, trying to figure out who we are. I'm still navigating learning who my biological family is, and there is beauty in it all. I can say today as a woman in her 40s, that God can answer prayers about family, no matter how difficult the situation.

I remember praying for this as a child, and receiving the answer as an adult did not diminish the power it had on my heart and life. It was nice to know my history so I could build from a solid foundation of who I am and grow to become. I enjoyed the time it took to learn each new family member, and I wouldn't change a thing in our journey. Giving my history to my children, for me, was an incredible gift, and I think it helped them achieve too, because they had more examples of what our family had accomplished in life. My dream had come true; now it was my children's turn!

My son was always passionate about real estate growing up, and it does my heart good to see him still pursuing it. He currently works in construction and is learning the ins and outs of building. My daughter is in school to become a Medical Assistant (MA) and use her gift of compassion to help others. They both always had a heart to love people like how I do as a social worker. I am so proud of them. We are very close, and I thank God that I can say I am the mother to them that I truly desired.

Monae is doing CNA work now as she continues school. It's funny to think of how much they have grown as I write this book. I remember one time when Monae and Chordae were growing up, Monae was maybe four or something like that at the time. She got a bright idea to take the bread tie, made of paper and wire, and stick it into the electrical socket. I heard a loud pop, and I don't remember if something happened temporarily with the power, but the noise from my children told me something was happening. When I ran upstairs, all I could smell was burnt toast.

I knew it when I saw their faces and smelled the singe of flesh; my daughter had been electrocuted. I instantly thought my son had put her up to it, and as I began to reprimand him for getting his sister shocked, he said, "She did it." When I asked him, "What did you do to your sister?"

I was so scared at that moment because I wasn't sure if she had done some serious damage to herself. She appeared to be alright, and we all laugh about it today when we remember the smell and things, but it was crazy for me at the time. I thought about whether I should put this in the book or not, but I had to share how sometimes the things that scare us, after we survive them, can make us laugh for years to come.

I also have to mention my bonus babies, who have been a joy and a wonderful surprise in my life. My bonus children are three boys named RJ, Terrell, and Jayden. They are 22, 18, and 12. RJ is a Gemini like me. Our birthdays are only a day apart, so I get him even when I don't wanna get him, I get him.

Terrell is 18, and he is going through the motions of becoming an adult. He is sharp, handsome, and thoughtful, and I know he will make the right decisions concerning his future. He has big plans, and I am excited for what he decides.

Lastly, I have my baby Jayden, who's 12. Jayden is in the middle school phase. Not quite a teenager or preteen, but quickly approaching it. He is learning about his friends, and friendships are becoming more important to him. All three of my bonus babies are so different, and I love seeing their growth and personalities.

RJ is really sweet, kind, and understanding, and Terrell is always helpful and resourceful in everything he does. Jayden is also very helpful, and he's kind. All three of them are really thoughtful, and I am sure they are picking up these traits from their father. It's so much fun to have all of these funny teenagers and growing adults in my life.

## Starting a Family

Jayden is very sociable and the talker of the family. He is athletic and loves basketball. I can understand why he loves the NBA and hopes to have a future in basketball for college or pro. He is a very good player with a good heart, and I am sure his hard work will pay off.

He loves basketball, but he also plays other sports and does everything boys his age enjoy. RJ definitely wants to go into a career for helping people and taking care of people who have behavioral and special needs. Terrell, at some point, wants to go into the Navy or Air Force.

I think they all have bright futures, and I think our family is, like, a great blend. I compare our family to a good pot of beef stew. We got carrots, potatoes, onions, and some of the best seasoning, with some bonus stuff in there. We have the meat, the foundation that makes a good family.

You do know that beef stew is not just about the beef, but everything in between. You gotta have the broth and the seasonings and stir the pot to mix it all in as it cooks to perfection. It must have that added heat and pressure to have the right taste. As you know, it takes a while to get your beef stew to taste the way you like it. I think it's a perfect example for our family, because it took some time for us to get here. It was never hard for us to get along, per se, but it took time for us to learn from each other.

We all love each other. But now, we just know more of why we choose to love each other. Love is a choice. I also had to learn that I don't need to feel love to extend love in those hard moments. It blesses our hearts to see everyone getting along so well and being there for each other. In the beginning, it took some time to get used to sharing each other's space for sure, and adapting to everyone's personalities, but we wouldn't choose it to be any other way.

It was that very same gentle introduction to everyone's differences and adjustments that laid a good foundation for my husband and I to want another baby. We wanted our family to grow and have a child that we could share together and could share with our children. We wanted to blend and create a baby who would have the benefit of all of our strengths combined.

All of our children would play a role in the life of Miracle, and our plan is to expand our family. It takes a village to raise a child, and our children were the first members of our village. We will love them all, always, no matter what comes; they have a permanent place in our hearts. We are grateful for how welcoming and supportive they were as we started our IVF journey, during the pregnancy, and after the birth of Miracle.

My husband and I were secure in our decisions to be together and build a union established in love, and that's also what we wanted to share with Miracle. It was with love and good intentions that our family started this journey to IVF.

*Monica Quarles*

# IVF JOURNEY

Alright, now we arrive at my IVF journey. A little bit about IVF, the acronym stands for In Vitro Fertilization (IVF), which is the joining of a woman's egg and a man's sperm in a petri dish. The word in vitro means outside the body. Fertilization, of course, means the sperm has attached to and entered the egg. Okay, now back to our journey.

Things were great at home, and it made the perfect environment to welcome another baby to our family. My husband and I really wanted this baby because she would be a bridge that further cemented our family together. So Robert and I wanted another baby because we wanted to have a love child. We wanted to have a child of our own, where, for the first time in our lives, as older adults, we could see the hand of God and the beauty of creating a family.

With my other pregnancies, I had to get with the program. I didn't take the time to plan out anything, but I reacted to the news. This experience was very different because of that. It was like another opportunity, another chance to do it right. After raising our older children, we felt we got some things right. If we had one more shot, perhaps we could be perfect! We didn't wanna be cheated out of knowing how much we can pour out as parents now that we are more mature and experienced, you know?

We both came from parents who were married. Both of us had active parents in the church who were Christians, believed in God, and had Christian values. This marriage was the first for both of us where we had a spouse who shared our same Christian values. And now we felt like we were in a situation where we could see the progress in how our children were being raised in this co-parenting and blended family. So we said, "Let's give it a try."

The only problem we had was that my tubes were tied. The only option for us that made sense was IVF, because getting my tubes untied would have been more traumatic because of my skin condition and the healing process. My body doesn't heal properly after major surgeries or injuries, so I didn't feel comfortable risking it. We educated ourselves on the IVF process, and we decided to go for it.

IVF has risks, and it doesn't always work. There are a lot of emotions that go into the mix, and a whole lot of prayer because you don't want to waste money and time. IVF is not normally an expense covered by insurance, so you have to pay out of pocket. I would have loved for my job or my husband's to cover the bill at least in part, but we paid it all ourselves.

We did the first treatment of IVF in 2021. This process cost us $30,000, and unfortunately, the first go round was not successful. After our first trial of IVF, we experienced firsthand how emotionally charged and overwhelming it really is. As hopeful parents, we wanted the good news more than we even realized. We put up the money, adjusted our lives financially and otherwise to support our vision. To then come up empty-handed, hurt real bad.

I was grateful that outside of my husband, I had other friends who were willing to offer their support during our process. I also found out that we were not alone in this journey and felt that our story should be shared with other parents. In light of that, we decided to start a YouTube channel on our IVF journey. Neither one of us are big on being consistent with social media. It wasn't our idea to start this channel but our children's idea.

They were all very supportive during the process and while we taped the Youtube series. It was nice to have them involved and supporting us through this journey because our decision to do IVF impacted all of us. I wanted to give my wonderful husband a baby girl because he had three boys and we had one daughter and four boys. We needed some help and a baby girl would be so perfect.

Of course, if we had a son together we would have been equally happy. Our biggest concern was to have a healthy baby more than we cared about the gender of the child. My husband and I wanted a girl, but we were okay with having a baby together no matter the outcome. This was something we decided and were going to do it together.

I didn't realize before starting IVF, the challenges that so many women face out there concerning infertility. I felt like for that brief moment in time, which felt like an eternity, I was able to relate to women that were wanting to conceive desperately, and it did not work out for them. It wasn't because they didn't pray enough, try hard enough, believe in it, or any of that.

I learned in this season of my life, there are many women who feel the disappointment and heartbreak we felt when we read about not being pregnant a few short weeks after our first round of IVF. My heart goes out to women who have been trying to conceive and it hasn't happened. I know how we can take our gift of children for granted, and I did some soul searching in those months of IVF.

I was thankful to my friend Mari, who shared her doctor's story with us when we were getting low and starting to feel like it wouldn't happen for us. We put our faith in Jesus to make this pregnancy happen. The science in IVF is very compelling, but we had a whole lot of Jesus and a little bit of science supporting our desire to become pregnant.

When I discovered IVF communities and groups, I joined them too. I needed to stay positive about our situation. I also needed to start taking medication to ensure the best results and to continue my health. I had to inject myself and take pills daily. The birth control I was on prior, I had to stop. My body was being challenged from every side, but I remained steadfast in my faith in God.

I was all in, and full of faith. I remember thinking, "Come on. Not again." You know how you have everything set up to be a great time, and here comes the rain to rain on your parade. I didn't want that to happen here. We had the money, the love, the right man and woman, God, so everything looked good.

Inside the groups I had joined and during the

Youtube podcast, I shared how I felt inadequate after IVF failed. I wanted to give my husband something that only I could do, and I had failed. It was devastating, and I shared my shame in the videos. I didn't realize how therapeutic blogging had become for me–even functioning as an outlet to let out my emotions.

The feedback from the comments and conversations was tremendous. I needed to be filled back up because I was in a dark place. I was depressed and heartbroken. I wanted to do all that I could to keep away from negative thoughts or disappointment. So to help change my mood, my husband and I traveled, and he did everything in his power to make me happy. My children also became extremely thoughtful and helpful towards me because they knew the results broke me on the inside.

I was bitter in every facet of life. I didn't give up on God, but I questioned his plan for my life, and I definitely wasn't that same warm and loving woman. It was hard to express myself and be truly authentic because these wounds were deep. I tried to hide from myself and others. Everyone wanted to talk, but I felt that they hardly listened to me. I know my husband didn't feel different towards me, but I was feeling ashamed and perplexed on every side.

I wondered how he could love me so much and live with the reality that I may not be able to give him a baby. I thought that giving him a baby would be the icing on the cake, but there was nothing baking but disappointment, frustration, and anger. I had accomplished so many things when I was ill-prepared and financially not ready, and to finally get married to my Mr. Right, have the right job, house, and setup, then fumble the ball to give him a baby just did not seem fair to me.

I mean, what kind of ending is to go through everything that I have been through in my previous marriages and being unwed and finally wedding and not being able to bear a child of our own. It was hard to look him in the face. I felt like we wasted our time and money. I really began to spiral and was unable to stop my mind from thinking the worst kind of thoughts.

I feel like the enemy was taunting me all over again telling me I was just not worthy, and it wasn't meant for me to have my happily ever after. I became bitter, and confused about what the purpose was and why we needed to go through such a tremendous heartbreak. I know in my soul that this was hard for my husband, but he felt like he needed to be strong for me. I admire that about him, but it made me even more sad that I couldn't give him a baby.

While I was on screen encouraging other women, I was shrinking inside. I had to get into counseling because this experience was bringing me to a place that was lower than I had ever been before. I was lost and searching for what I could not find. I needed to shake these emotions and if you are feeling like I was, I cannot stress enough how important it is to invest in you. Counseling is for you and all those you love.

The vacations and counseling helped me to come out of my depression. I wasn't 100% me, but I would say 80%. I remember one day when we were laughing and talking, he got quiet and looked me in my eyes gently and said, "We gotta go back for our baby. Right?" I just sat there looking at him as my smile switched to a withdrawn gaze. I looked like a deer caught in the headlights, I was terrified. I didn't think I could go through that again.

And he said, "You know, we can't leave our baby there." He said it with such conviction and love. I was still not feeling it, but I wanted to make my husband happy. He had enough faith for the both of us because I didn't have any faith that this time would be different than the first time. I wanted it to be, but I couldn't handle the heartbreak if it did not work.

My husband was so excited and his excitement made me smile through the process. He helped me to push away my own fears and doubts; I trusted the smile that got me this far. It felt like I was running back into a burning building after I barely escaped the first time. I remember saying to myself, "I never want to do this again."

But my husband was right. We had two embryos left at the doctor's office. And I remember the day of the retrieval. I didn't want to have my emotions too high and I tried to treat this like an ordinary doctor's visit–but I knew it was not. I felt like something was off and I told the doctor, "Something's wrong."

The doctor was always early for any appointment we had and he would encourage us that everything will be fine. He told us, "One of the eggs didn't make it." I knew what he meant but it didn't make me feel confident at all. I was trying not to read into it, but allow what the Father's will is to be what happens.

"Everything's gonna be okay, Monica," he told me reassuringly as I gathered my thoughts for our second round of IVF. I replied, "It only takes one. Right?" I was trying to encourage myself, and maybe the doctor too because this was our last shot. The first round of IVF was $30,000 and the second was $6,000.

As I lay there undergoing the procedure, that day, I wasn't able to see anything on the screen. It was like a day that I had never experienced in the doctor's office before, even unlike our previous visit for IVF. I had to have that same blind faith all over again that this would work.

After everything was done, I remember saying to my husband, "Ready to go get some fries?" The doctor and my husband laughed and their response brought lightness back into the room. I am glad it stopped being so heavy. They joked about my appetite for McDonald's fries, and as they joked, I silently prayed to God to help this work because I couldn't handle another failure.

A few days later, I started to feel sick. I wasn't sure what kind of sickness this was, because it wasn't like a normal pregnancy really–but nothing about this process was. I remember my numbers being super low to test if I was pregnant or not, so many weeks had to gone by before the results would be accurate.

It was so scary and discouraging. It was hard to pull through this season and keep my stress level down. To make matters a bit worse, our teenagers were at each other's throats, and the family dynamic was not as warm as before.

It was nothing we couldn't manage and get through but the timing of it was hard on me for sure. Their grades were dropping and they were struggling socially outside the home. As we were dealing with other family dynamics, I had to keep telling myself, try to stay calm. I was trying to keep my stress managed because I couldn't risk complications with this pregnancy.

For weeks, I went through testing because my beta

numbers were low. Hearing the conclusion of my results, with everything else, it was weighing on me. My husband was there to ease my mind, but it was me and God who had to work it out. I called on the name of Jesus often because me and my family needed him.

Then finally, I asked, " Am I pregnant? Yes or no?" Then they told me, "Congratulations Monica and Robert, you are pregnant." Then it hit me, wow! We are pregnant! It worked. I was overjoyed and nervous. I wasn't feeling well for weeks, and it looked like the morning sickness would continue because I was pregnant. I couldn't believe it.

In the first trimester, I was sick the whole time. Brushing my teeth was just, like, icky. I could barely eat, I was sick, and throwing up a lot. It was the hardest pregnancy. Morning sickness lasted much longer than my prior pregnancies. It practically lasted the entire duration of my pregnancy.

Although I was putting on pounds, my baby wasn't advancing as much. She didn't meet the expectations for weight, length, and other benchmarks in the womb. I was measuring fine, but she wasn't. The first and second trimester was still uneventful, but the third showed more alarming news in the ultrasounds.

As we looked at the screen and saw the whispering of the techs, we knew something wasn't quite right. The doctor later confirmed that there was an issue they could see with some of her organs. It looked like her heart could have a hole in it, but nothing more was discussed.

Other causes for alarm continued to pop up on the radar, and the doctors thought to check my stress levels. Our baby wasn't breathing on her own as needed to pass the test, so they were troubleshooting why. I am no doctor, but I could just feel like something wasn't right with our baby. I remember having frantic prayers, like, "Please let my baby be healthy in Jesus' name. And Jesus, Jesus, Jesus, please don't let nothing be wrong with my baby." I couldn't shake the feeling I felt about the situation, although I prayed it wasn't the truth.

Being sick my entire pregnancy did not make me alarmed right away. I was going through the motions of being pregnant and I just didn't feel good. All we could do was keep praying and believing that God would take us through this. We couldn't focus too much on what the ultrasound said and what could be, we had to keep going down this journey of faith.

My husband loved bonding with baby Miracle in the womb. He was present for all of the doctor's appointments, ultrasounds, and loved to talk to the baby through my stomach. He was fathering her from the womb. Miracle would respond to him with movements, kicking, and I just wanted to hear his voice. Their bond started before she was born.

It is a beautiful thing to see a father and daughter relationship like theirs. My husband and our daughter have always been connected and it is warming to know I wasn't in this alone. We were excited that IVF worked and whenever I had a rough day, he was good to remind me of our journey thus far. We didn't know anything for sure about the ultrasound, many things were educated guesses they felt they should tell us in case.

Miracle stayed in positions that made it difficult to know what was really going on in there. So we all had to wait. The only red flags I had about the pregnancy was how I felt and how this pregnancy differ so greatly from my other two. I just had a woman's intuition that something was wrong although I didn't know what.

There were a lot of people around during IVF time and I was very grateful for them. I expected them to be around still as the delivery date drew closer, but, oh, soon did that change.

*Monica Quarles*

*Monica Quarles*

# BIRTH STORY

Leading up to the day of birth, gosh, I was so tired. My body was hurting, and I was barely getting any sleep. And I was still throwing up. I remember, May 8th, I was at my wit's end about being pregnant.

I remember saying to myself, "I am over this. I'm gonna do the midwife's brew tea to help me go into labor." So I drank this concoction. I walked and walked around the downtown Indianapolis State Building, up and down any stairs I could find, and anywhere close to urge along labor.

I literally walked until my body couldn't walk anymore. I remember having contractions while sitting on the couch. I started to time them with my husband. I remember talking with my mother-in-law when she came over about my progress. I got in the tub that night not so much to push along labor, but to ease my now sore limbs.

But I guess all the walking and tea I had ingested started to kick in later that evening. It was about 8pm when my contractions started to come in real strong. We ended up calling the midwife because the contractions were pretty steady. The midwife came and she checked my cervix, and told me that Miracle was not in the right position.

She told me to lay in the doggy style position for about forty five minutes to an hour, and she would check my cervix again. I remember seeing a little blood clot or something after she had checked me. I thought that could have been my bloody show, but soon enough I would be sure. The midwife felt like I wasn't in active labor yet, but going through a false alarm based on my cervix and progress.

"It could be a couple of days before your baby is here. Try to be patient and give your body a rest. I will be back in a day or so to check on you again then." She didn't feel I wasn't at my pain point yet, and thought that pains were simply pregnancy related and not signs of active labor. After a hour, she decided to go home with a smile.

The night was getting late and maybe we were coming down from the excitement of expecting our baby to arrive that night. I was in bed at about 10:30pm and I just laid there. The pains didn't go away completely, and my pain level had jumped a few notches by 11pm. She told me to try and sleep, but I couldn't. I was in more pain now than before.

My contractions were coming hard and fast, so fast that I could barely breathe. My husband was like, "Breathe Monica." I'm like, "I can't breathe, I can't breathe. Breathe..." Then I just remember jumping off the bed, like, "Oh my God."

Now, I was in a panic, because I was just told an hour previously that I was not in active labor, and if not, what is this pain coming from? It definitely felt like labor to me. The kids were home and trying to go to sleep. They were still in school at the time, and I knew that this night would be a night that they would never forget. Now, I am trying to calm down, so I started playing worship music. It wasn't but a handful of seconds into the song that I was like, "Turn it off. I can't, I can't focus."

I told my husband, "I wanna go to the hospital." I quickly changed my mind about a home birth and wanted to go to the hospital. The pain was so intense that I was overcome by it. I kept calling on God to help me through it and get me to the hospital. But the precious time I spent waiting to calm down was the brief hours I would spend in labor.

I realized quickly I wasn't making it to the hospital. This baby was coming, and she was determined to be born now. I was going to have our baby right there at the house.

We had planned to have a home birth, but not this way. I wanted to give birth in the tub, this was not the plan, and I was so frantic. It was so hard to calm me down. Everybody was in flight mode: the children, my husband, and I. We were all in shock I think, and all I kept saying was, "Oh my goodness."

I wasn't in labor very long, considering my previous pregnancies. I was in labor with my oldest son for twenty-four hours, and I was in labor with my oldest daughter for twelve. With Miracle, I was literally in labor for maybe three hours. And so I just got to the point where I kneeled down and I said, "I have to push!"

The urgency came over me, and I was squatting in front of our bed, in front of the TV. The kids were just there, amazed and probably fearful, because I'm just hollering in pain. I just remember a gush of fluid coming out with the last push. On May 9, 2023 at 2:40 am, my husband delivered his daughter. When I pushed, he caught her in his hands, and I think I kinda blacked out for a moment. I remember my husband telling me shortly after I delivered Miracle that she wasn't breathing. I heard them calling her name and patting her back to wake her up.

I was in a daze. And then he put her on my chest, and I just fell in love immediately. After all those emotions had calmed down, he called the midwife back and said, "I delivered my baby! She is here." They came over within the hour, and we didn't cut the umbilical cord while we waited. It was a perfect time of bonding with our baby and holding her and just thanking God that she came out, and we did it together.

Although it was a lot to endure, I enjoyed that our children were there for the birth. This moment brought us all together, and seeing my daughter, son, and bonus children there for us in those moments is something we will never forget. The birth of Miracle will always be a very special memory.

I was shocked and in disbelief for a long while after everything happened. My body went through all those changes, and without the help of a midwife or a hospital. When the midwives came to evaluate us, they said that Miracle was tongue-tied and lip-tied. So they clipped her tongue and her lip. So from day one, she had to be strong, and she was.

She was very, very, little, and I fell in love with my tiny but mighty Miracle. It was love at first sight. I didn't go to the hospital right away either. I started to notice, in the days ahead, that Miracle's eyes were a little yellow, which I had never seen before. I had really never known anything about jaundice because my previous deliveries didn't have any problems with jaundice. I just remember after birth wanting a break from medical staff and people. But when I thought about the changes she had already undergone, I paid a bit more attention to looking at her. When I did, I noticed it was like a lump or hole in her neck. I wasn't too sure what it was, so I decided to go to the hospital.

Normally, the baby would see the midwife in the early days of care, but I wasn't sold on their knowledge. After the birth and my feeling of a mistake they made to have me deliver alone, I thought more professional help might be best. Even during my pregnancy, I wasn't 100% sold on midwife care alone.

I had always had an OB/GYN monitoring me the whole pregnancy, while I was going to the midwife, just in case I chose a hospital birth last minute. But when I realized there were things that were going on with my daughter that they could have missed, I immediately took her to the doctor and started to see what was going on.

In the beginning, my husband had time off, so he was there for the testing. He was attending the appointments with me, and we were going through the test together. He was a great support, and seeing how he bonded with Miracle when she was first born, I knew it set the tone for their relationship. He has been committed to her needs since before she was born.

I think when I went to the first doctor that I chose, she was very concerned that my daughter's weight was an issue. I think that was another indicator that something serious would soon be discovered. So, alongside being lip- and tongue-tied, she was not gaining weight. When we were going to those weekly checkups following her birth, her birth weight was very low. And I was nursing, but Miracle really did not nurse well.

I tried to put her in some therapies to get her some help there. The center that specializes in home births also provided assistance with helping babies nurse. I tried those services to see how they could help Miracle, but after a few sessions, we knew that wasn't helping either. We had a problem and we needed to sort it out. They did help us with some things we could use, but the main problem was still there.

It was when we were trying to sort out her feeding that the pediatrician noticed the heart murmur. Latching on for Miracle was really tough. It was painful for me, and a challenge for her. I nursed briefly with my oldest daughter, and it was in my heart to do things better for Miracle. I was learning about all the benefits from the center for breastfeeding, and I wanted to give her my best.

It was at the cardiologist office that my daughter's life changed, but I was so grateful to know what was really going on. Finding out that her bilirubin numbers were high, helped to explain the problems we were having with feeding. It takes a village to treat a child with special needs, and I am grateful for all the help we got in her first few weeks of life even up until now.

We found at the hospital appointment she was jaundiced. They said it might have been missed because she's African American, and that makes it harder for doctors to detect so they often miss it. The hospital doctor referred us to the best cardiologists and I am forever grateful for that. Both teams saved Miracle's life, but especially her cardiologists.

The cardiologist urged us, as we walked out the door, to head to the hospital afterward. What we thought was going to be an appointment to address her being juandiced, turned into an 8-day stay at the hospital, where we learned that Miracle was diagnosed with Alagille Syndrome. Alagille Syndrome (ALGS) is a rare disorder that affects multiple organs, most notably the liver, heart, eyes, bones, and other organs. It's characterized by a reduced number of bile ducts in the liver, leading to cholestasis (reduced bile duct flow) and liver damage. ALGS affects other systems, including the cardiovascular, skeletal, and renal systems, and can cause distinctive facial features and delays in growth and development. Miracle was 6 weeks old when she was diagnosed with a rare disease.

Another thing the doctors pointed out was this cleft palate on the side of her neck. We got it looked at and they said, "Basically, it's just some extra skin that some kids are born with. It shouldn't cause any problems, but if it gets too big, we can have it surgically removed."

They went on to say they would keep monitoring it, but for now, don't worry too much about it. They were right, I had no time to worry about that when so many other tests and blood draws were happening to test for different potential issues. Bringing Miracle home from the doctor's appointments and emerging her into the family circle posed its own set of challenges.

*Monica Quarles*

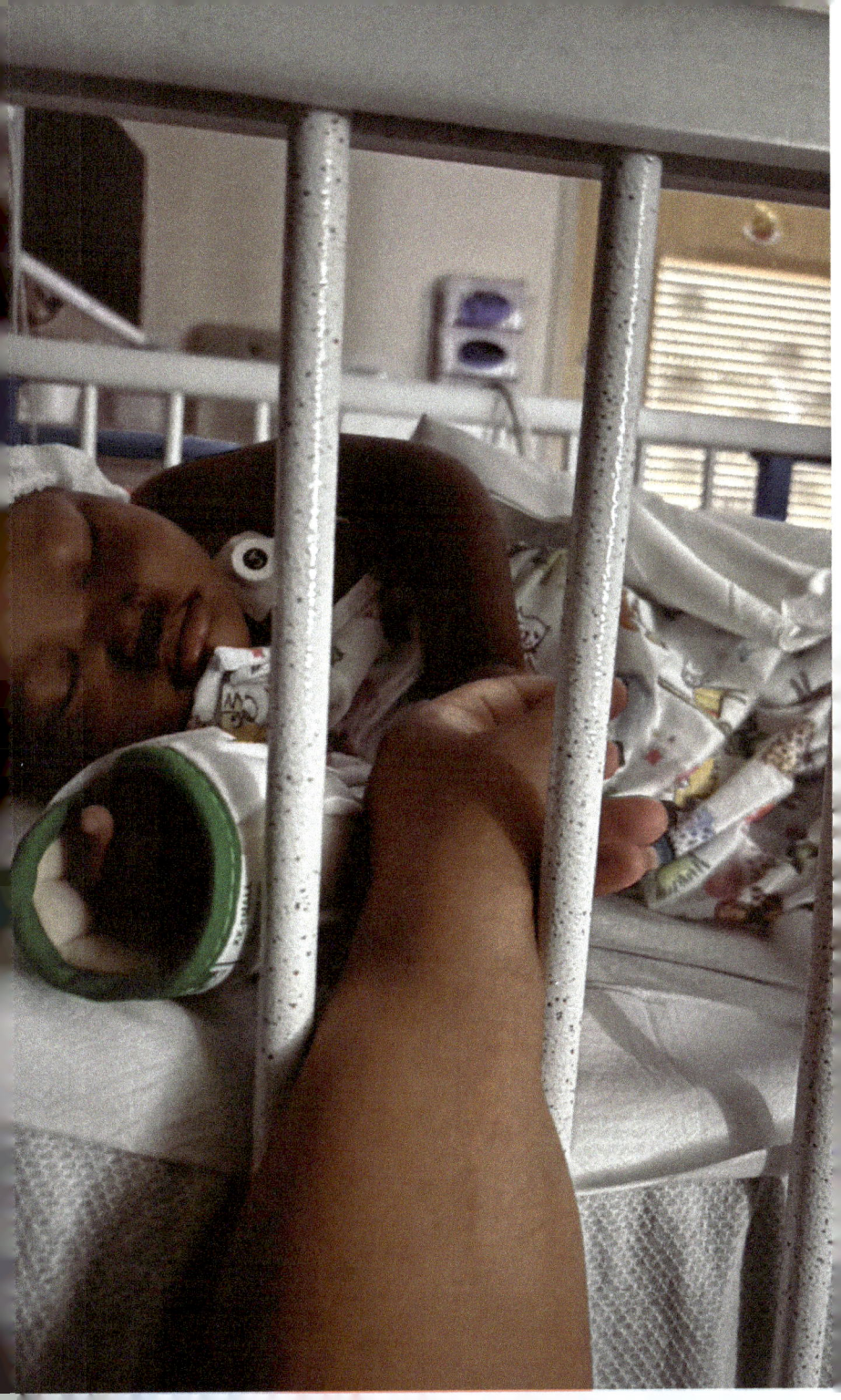

*Monica Quarles*

# MIRACLE ARRIVES HOME

Miracle arrives home and I can tell you that it was pure joy, holding a baby that me and my husband brought into this world was bliss. We had journeyed and got through the process of IVF to be here. It was so special. I was so tired and ready to get my body back, like after any pregnancy. I will say that my labor was very short and I think that was because Miracle wanted out too. She wanted to see the faces and match the voices she heard with a pair of eyes and a warm smile.

The look on my husband's face as he looked at our daughter was priceless. You can just see the love all over his face. The children were happy too when baby Miracle arrived home. She brought a calm storm to our home that we all needed. We needed to get out of our own way and focus on someone who needed us more than our stresses.

It was wonderful to share this experience with her grandmothers and great grandmothers who came over on the first day she was home. They smiled at her and marveled at the creation God gave us. The newest member of the family was here and she was beautiful to see. I could get some rest when they arrived because I knew she was in good hands.

Great aunts also came to see her when she first arrived and it felt warm to see them. The door didn't stop revolving when Miracle first arrived. My three sisters came to make an appearance, also. Although we were overjoyed with all of the support, I was also a bit overwhelmed. I wasn't prepared for all the company, but I think because I had the baby in such an untraditional way, everybody just swarmed to my house in the same way. Nothing about Miracle's story has been normal so I can see why everyone was so quick to support us on the first day.

To be honest, I had wished that I was more vocal about what I wanted. I would have loved to get used to my change at my own pace and invite others into that space when I was ready. I didn't say much about people coming and dropping by, but I really wished I had. I needed some time to heal and adjust. Not getting that, I felt like I was behind and in some kind of whirlwind I couldn't get out of.

The hospital put a boundary in place to where people knew they couldn't just flood your room, but at home, you are in a comfortable space so people feel more comfortable about visiting. I would have liked to have had a similar boundary in place just long enough for me to rest and catch up with life. I think my husband could have used the time also so we didn't feel like we had to entertain others and share the moment too soon with our extended family.

It wasn't that I didn't want any visitors, but we had so many, it was hard to catch up. Because I was in my bed, but also sharing and entertaining, I didn't recover. On the other hand, I am very grateful to be able to tell her when she is older how everyone supported her since day one by coming to see her. I was tired, but they wanted to share their love and I needed to be patient and open to it. I am glad that we all had the experience, regardless of the inconvenience; it is very special to me.

Miracle slept for the first month. Feeding didn't go so well because she wasn't able to latch on. Like in the womb, she didn't eat much. She was hungry but had no appetite. I didn't sleep much because I was a nervous wreck. It was like being a new mom all over again, and Miracle wasn't eating. My husband took a leave from work to be there with me for the first few weeks after her birth, and our children really helped me a lot. The family bonding time was very heartfelt, and I am grateful to them all for helping to make my job as a mom lighter.

I was off work, and it felt good to rest, even if it was intermittent, to spend time with Miracle. The lack of sleep over time began to wear on me as she got older, and my body craved more sleep. I think after a couple of weeks of not sleeping, I started to feel postpartum kicking in. At first, I didn't know what was keeping me from getting myself together. It felt laborious to get dressed, do my hair, or think of anything outside of what I was dealing with at the time.

My everyday life was spent being concerned about our new miracle. She didn't take a bottle, and at birth, she had complications that made nursing difficult. I didn't really pump much, not sure if my body wasn't made for milking, or if I was too stressed to eat and produce enough. It was all hard. I was struggling with breastfeeding, but I managed to do it for 2 years despite my initial complications. I was growing frustrated with not being able to feed my baby and help her get the proper nutrients she needed.

I felt like I was failing her, and I didn't really catch

a lot of her hunger cues because she didn't really seem to have them. I tried timing her meals, but she ate on her own schedule. I would try to get her on a schedule for feeding, diaper changes, playing with her, and still, at times, she wasn't happy. I'm like, she should be eating right about now, but she didn't eat very much. You would hear her lips smacking for a few minutes, like, oh, that's good. Then she was done.

My husband still had to work and needed his rest. He tried to be there with me and spend time with Miracle, but I took on the full-time role. And I realized, I became consumed in a way with Miracle. She was my baby, and she was my primary focus. She was my first love, and everything else became secondary. I needed balance, but wasn't sure of how to get it.

I was very worried and overprotective of her. I just had a lot of anxiety surrounding Miracle because she wasn't growing. I wasn't sure of how fragile she might be with how little weight gain she had. I knew she didn't eat much, and I didn't want someone else to grow frustrated with her. I know it is not easy to know what a baby should eat when they choose not to eat.

Going to those appointments was pretty tough, because it was like, "Yeah, she didn't gain very much weight. Let's try to get her to eat a little bit more." And I'm like, she just isn't showing those signs of hunger. She never had much of an appetite. She is just not a big eater. But what she loves is getting dolled up like any little girl. I loved bathing her, getting her dressed, and combing her hair. All those little girl things little babies liked to do, she loves.

She wasn't a big crier, and she had the tiniest voice. I

just love her so much. I was just so overjoyed and happy when she came, but worried at the same time. It was so crazy to have all those mixed emotions all into one, but they were all present. Miracle had my attention, and really, she had all of our attention. Miracle's arrival was monumental, to say the least.

*Monica Quarles*

*Monica Quarles*

# PPD

I think postpartum depression can kick in when you feel the weight of the world on your shoulders. It doesn't mean you are alone or you don't care or appreciate those around you. I had a wonderful husband who was there for me through this entire process, who was still attracted to me, showing his love for me and our new baby, but I was struggling to keep up.

It was hard for me to adjust to the needs of Miracle and her surgeries, with other problems calling for my attention. I still had to mother the rest of the children in our house and be a wife, all while Miracle demanded lots of my attention and emotional strength. I was going through the motions, but some daily tasks I struggled to complete, like getting out of bed sometimes.

Miracle has undergone several surgeries. I remember her surgery on March 26th, 2024, when she got her G tube placed. It was a hard thing to see my daughter have to resort to a procedure because she was unable to eat. Before the G tube, she had an NG tube that was placed down her nose and down her stomach to help with eating; this lasted three months and didn't work.

I wanted this to be a temporary thing. I hoped it would not be something I would have to do or she would have to experience for an extended period of time. I wanted our circumstances to change, and after seeing that they were not, it did something to me. That was hard for me, and the journey ahead for our family is still hard.

After the G tube was placed, it was something that changed my spirit. I was in a dark place and felt like I was out of control of everything. I think in a way I internalized her care as my failure, being that it was something I was helpless to change. This mindset really worked on my emotions and drained my energy.

I wasn't sure of the real source of how I realized I needed help with postpartum depression. I wasn't sure if it dawned on me because I was unavailable for my other growing children. It was hard for me to be present for them, and not because I didn't want to be. I know sometimes those impacted by postpartum depression can think your depression is because of them.

I love all of my children and none of them is a choice that I regret. When I reached this place, my children were not to blame. I can't help but wonder if they started to blame themselves or searched for blame as to why I was suffering. The truth, I don't think my suffering was linked to any one person, it was just an experience happening inside of me.

I was trying to process my pressure, thinking, wants, and desires. I had to learn to deal with the fact that some of the things I wanted, I wasn't getting. I kept trying to say I was alright when my husband asked, but he knew that I wasn't. He was so intentional with making sure I was present for everyone and knew I was loved. His patience with me and my children is something I am forever grateful for.

It was very difficult for us to be close and spend intimate time together because, you know, we really needed to pick our time wisely when we did not have Miracle. So a lot of the time when we took breaks, it was to handle more business and more responsibility, not really thinking that our marriage is a huge responsibility in itself.
I feel like I didn't have a lot of time for myself, my husband, my other kids, my life, and I questioned who I was becoming.

When I was unable to get out of bed, or hardly able to talk, or show affection, he tried to understand. But I struggled to see things from his perspective. I couldn't empathize at the time with anyone else's feelings because I was absorbed in mine. I didn't want to be this way, but I wasn't sure of how not to be.

I think I had been coasting for a very long time on depression, feeling overwhelmed because I wasn't sure of how to see myself after a while, aside from all of my responsibilities. I was losing that funny, happy-go-lucky, light version of myself. I just remember the days when I did not wanna get out of bed after I got Miracle together. I would get her dressed, comb her hair, and clean up her throw-up by washing the sheets. I was tired after completing these tasks.

But it wasn't just the tasks that triggered depression, I think it was my age also. I was now 40 years old with a baby. I had adult kids. And, I started to think, what in the world did I do? Like, what happened? What was happening to me?

I felt like I had my life altogether and figured out, but that all changed in the blink of an eye. The balance of home life with the children turned into more fights.

The loving marriage was becoming withdrawn, and my sense of self was erasing. I didn't know what to do as I sat through each day with my thoughts, trying to process my emotions. The reality of my choices set in, and I needed help to escape the loop I was in. It was then that I sought help. I told my husband one day when he asked, "You know, hey. I am not okay," with tears running down my face.

It is really tough to know if you are really okay or not when there is so much that can change in a moment. It can be hard to avoid the what-ifs and the things you hope don't happen when you read things that paint a different picture. Going to doctor's appointments and hearing the percentages and side effects of any and everything that impacts you. This was part of the weight that triggered my depression, my daughter's diagnosis.

I remember my husband being very candid with me and telling me, "No, we are not going to think like this. I know that this is hard for us. But nothing is too hard for God. We are going to just trust God. I know that God knows how to take care of our baby, Miracle."

He just always told me she was gonna be okay. After the surgery, I knew in my heart that she was gonna be okay. But it was overwhelming sometimes, just looking at what was in front of you. It's hard to look past what you see and put your faith in it. My faith was struggling because when I would pray and stand on what I prayed to come through, if it didn't, it made me second-guess a little bit.

It was like I saw the problem being magnified, and then my faith started lowering because it's like, okay, Lord, where are you at? I guess it's like when you need back up, or think you have it, and you start going for it, only to see that who you thought was gonna be there wasn't. But the truth, it wasn't that God wasn't there, but that he didn't operate in the way I expected him to. I thank God for a supportive and Godly husband who was unwavering in his faith and love for me during this difficult time. I love you baby.

I thought he was gonna show up as a healer, but that wasn't happening like I envisioned it. Like, whatever we think in our finite minds, we cannot grasp the things of God and why we go through what we go through. This process tends to create a lot of questions, and one being, "God, why?"

"Why do you think I'm strong enough for this?" I wasn't sure of the strength God knew I had, because to me, I was sinking. I was in a really dark spot, and I had to start going to counseling. I needed to get help, and it was time. It was definitely time.

I think a lot of us might feel like going to counseling is almost a form of failure and not success. I had to again stop leaning on my own understanding and learn to trust the process. God puts people on this earth to work together and encourage each other. We all have something to give and need something from others. Going to counseling helped me to talk to someone who was unbiased. I felt heard and listened to after each session. I didn't have to worry about, you know, somebody saying, "Girl, God's got it and this and that." I know the saying, and I believe, like all Christians, that God has the final say on how he will handle things.

But the other side of the coin, and the human thing to do, is to ask yourself, "What else can I do? How can I get myself back up from here?" And it was like the things that you need to get up and take care of yourself are simple. Like, it's impossible to take care of anyone else if you haven't given yourself any time, and I had put myself on the back burner. Everyone had a piece of me but me.

And, I mean, even God was on the back burner. I would say my prayers but even those were all about my children, Miracle's healing, and everyone else. My prayers stopped being about me and just talking to God because it was a pretty day. My prayers were dominated by Miracle's healing to the point I couldn't see that my marriage needed help. I couldn't see that my other kids were clearly having some behavior issues because this was a lot on them also.

This disease was evasive and can touch every part of our child's body. This disease is rare so not everything is known about it, and many things are in limbo. It feels like we are constantly reacting to solve problems and not being proactive. I think that's what I had hoped would be achieved through my prayers.

When that didn't seem to be working, I didn't understand the magnitude of my disappointment or hurt. My husband, not really familiar with depression, didn't really understand, but he wanted to be supportive. He told me to do whatever it was that I needed to do, to get some help, because I'm one of those people, like, oh, I got it. I got it, even if I don't have it.

I got the assignment, but I didn't have it. I didn't have the push. I didn't have the drive. I didn't wanna get out of bed. I didn't want to shower or bathe myself. I didn't wanna eat, but if I did, I was overeating. Have you ever been here before?

I just felt so secluded, and I couldn't share all of the different things that I was truly going through in my mind with anybody. So, yeah, I ended up going to counseling. My sessions were online because I didn't have a lot of time to get up out of the house and move around with Miracle's schedule. Also, I took partial leave when she got the G tube. I needed to take a step back from work to focus on how I was feeling and what I needed, too. I was glad I was able to give myself some time because of the help of others.

I didn't have to rush back to the workforce because I had support. During my time off, I was grateful for my neighbors stepping up tremendously to help my family through this time. They didn't charge me to watch Miracle when I needed them to. They helped with pick-ups and drop-offs I might have needed with my other children or running errands. They were all just very supportive, and that helped a lot to keep me encouraged.

At that time, we had also joined a new church that actually cared about us and fed us spiritually. I always knew a solid Bible Church was valuable, but at this point in my life, it was further solidified. This Bible-teaching church helped, like everything else, but if I was honest, I still felt low. I couldn't regulate my emotions, and I was struggling to focus on my daily tasks. I spoke to my counselor about it, and she recommended medication to help me through this difficult transition.

They prescribed me Zoloft, which I would take at night, and it was a safe product for nursing mothers. I felt kinda bad that I needed medicine to help me deal with things. Whenever I would feel down about it, I would quickly be reminded of how I needed this, and I had to care about my own well-being first. Everyone will have an opinion, but I would be the one having to live with my life's choices. I needed this medication to help me balance out my life and get back to a sense of normal.

I could tell a change was slowly happening when I was on the medication, and then when I was off. I was more hesitant when I didn't have it. I feel like in our culture, black culture, we're told that what goes on in your house stays in your house. We are championed for self-healing, no matter what kind of job we do.

Our community is quick to tell you, "You don't need to let nobody be in your business," but how else are you supposed to get help? I wasn't looking for pity, like some would imply. I heard the comments, "You gotta be strong, " like "I didn't have permission to have a weak moment," or "Girl, you gotta pick yourself up by your bootstraps," and it's like yeah, that's great advice until it's not." For me, I didn't want that; I wanted to feel heard.

People often assume that self-love and self-healing can be achieved alone, implying that you will never need anyone or anything to help guide you in this pursuit. I was pretending that I had it together, and I didn't realize it until I started talking. I had to learn that meeting everybody else's needs and forgetting your own is not really showing love. It's a poor representation of love because you must love yourself to love others. It was I who wasn't loving myself well.

I was so caught up in being what everyone else needed, I forgot how to be what I needed. When you are this depleted, you need more than just talking to somebody and a pat on the back. I needed counseling and medication, and I don't believe others who need to go this route should feel guilty about their journey to healing, just as I don't.

At this time, when I needed more, so did my baby. I was aware of the importance of breast milk and its status as the most nutritious supplement a baby can have. If you breastfeed a child for at least 8 months, their bodies build up way more antibodies than the children who didn't nurse for that long. I wanted to be the sole source for my baby's nutrition, knowing that I had what she needed. And I did–but she needed more than I could provide.

Yes, breast milk is the best source, but it is not always all a baby needs to thrive; sometimes they need extra. I didn't even want to give her formula and things like that, just because of some of the reviews I had heard about formula, but I was forced. There were some things that I was forced to do against my will because of my daughter's rare disease. I did not want to initially vaccinate my child because a lot of the vaccinations can cause medical issues or side effects.

But my convictions of not having her vaccinated were canceled when I was told she wouldn't be put on the liver transplant list unless she had all of her vaccinations and immunizations. I had to go back on a decision that I originally didn't want to change. In life, circumstances can make us change course and do what we said we wouldn't do. I wanted this pregnancy and early parenting experience to be different, mostly better, because I was more educated than in previous pregnancies. I didn't anticipate how different this experience would become.

I thought this part of my life would be bliss, but I found myself not only battling depression but also bitterness. I grew bitter, and I believe that was a contributing factor to why I needed medical help and additional support. I had rage and had nowhere to direct it. I wanted to blame someone or something, but I couldn't do that either, so maybe I was sulking in my pain.

Like how you need a shot of morphine and something to take your focus off an injured wound, so you can calm down and allow other work to be done to get well, I needed help to calm down and clear my head because my emotions were in overdrive. I was disappointed not just in myself, but if I am honest, with God, too. I wanted him to show up mighty in battle for me, but I was feeling let down with my daughter's ongoing sickness and how the rare disease spread to new issues.

This was not supposed to be the follow-up to a happy wedding day and the plans we created with God. This was not the storyline we prayed for or believed God to give us. We wanted a different experience with the same beautiful child included. We wanted her healthy, out of pain, and able to live a normal life.

And, you know, sometimes there's no right combination. Sometimes you just gotta be real and tell God how you feel because he can handle it. After I got out my emotions and thoughts, then I could see how God was able to change my heart and work to heal me. My reaction to disappointment wasn't on God, but on me. I needed to be open to allow God to love me and comfort me instead of isolating myself from him and everyone else.

I needed God to open me back up to being loved, so that I could love others better–including him. I went to counseling for 6 months and followed the assignments. I did the work because that was necessary to have what I really desired. I didn't want a perfect family because I believed the family I had was the right one. I had to accept that God didn't make any mistakes. I would be grateful for who I had in my life and pray for strength as I went through the process of loving my husband and raising our children.

I determined that I didn't really need counseling anymore or medication after I began to be honest about my feelings. I learned to better communicate with God and my husband. Being open to vent and express how I am feeling gave me the freedom I needed without the medication. It's okay to outgrow what you needed for a season. Crutches are meant to carry your weight until you are strong enough to stand on your own two legs again.

A block that I was able to break through to better communicate with my husband was realizing that talking to him about how I felt was not a burden to him. He works on the road driving large semis. I know the stress of the job and I didn't want to make his day worse with my problems. However, being silent about my problems only meant the small things grew to mountains forming stumbling blocks. I had to learn to put my weight on him when I needed him and trust the support system that he gave me.

Have you ever heard of the saying, "Sometimes you have to lose to win?" I had to lose my ideal of what I pictured my life to be to make room for what my life was. I had to grieve the life and vision I imagined in my own way. Grief is not only stirred up when someone physically dies, but also when an idea dies. My life wasn't all bad and it didn't get worse, but became much greater than I envisioned. I had to make room for the larger picture in my mind and in my heart.

For women going through postpartum depression, I would create a checklist to help you remember to think about yourself. Like I really want you to look at yourself in the mirror and be honest. I know it sounds a bit crazy, but trust this process. I had a list and I would ask myself questions.

### "Where am I? How am I doing?

### Am I bathing? Am I eating? Am I talking? Am I in my head all the time?

### Am I being honest with my family? Am I being honest with my friends? Am I giving myself grace?

Then I would say, ask for help and be open to counseling. Allow someone else to guide you through this journey like I did. It doesn't have to take you six months, and it could take more time, but so what? Your mental health is important because it impacts your physical health and those around you, too.

Next, be open to medication if needed. If you broke your leg, you may need crutches, a scooter, or a boot. All of these aids are designed to support you throughout your healing process.

I had to ask for more help from my husband to help balance my time. I needed to start taking naps with Miracle. When I needed rest, I had to ask my husband to fill in for me or my children. In the early months, I was with Miracle all the time and never once took a day off or went on vacation. I was scared to leave her with anyone. I had to overcome that and learn to ask God for help through it.

I had to trust the hands that were willing to help me with Miracle and not feel that I had to do it all by myself. If you are a person who typically doesn't like asking for help, this is not the time, because your child needs you, and you want to help your child. The best part is, everyone else wants what you want, but you have to open your mind more to see the bigger picture and not just your version of it.

I remember how even my coworkers started to help in ways they could. Help can come from all kinds of directions. Accept help when it is provided. When my children saw me crying, they were all moved to ask me, "Mom, what can I do?" At first, I didn't ask for a lot, but I learned to trust them all more and their ability to solve problems their way.

Lastly, I would like to say it is okay to love God, trust God, and still be scared. I was scared after seeing the post of children who died from the disease Miracle has. Reading the articles didn't function as a form of support, but fear. I wanted to change the fear I had into something positive, and that is what counseling helped me to do. It helped me to focus on the small things, because large accomplishments are achieved in the small things.

I had to learn to celebrate our success and not look so far ahead to the area of gray space, but to be in the moment. I wanted Miracle to be in the moment, too. I want her to enjoy being a child and knowing what it is like to be a baby. My therapy was shopping, and so Miracle had everything, especially when she was younger. I spared no expense to make sure she enjoyed every second of her life. But, I also have to ensure she is balanced and understands the same values my husband and I instilled in our other children.

Not everything we did before is bad or unworthy of passing on. It's okay to change, to evolve, and take life one day at a time. Embracing the day will help you become stronger to face whatever comes tomorrow. You get more organized. You remember things you forgot, and you are better able to focus when you slow down to breathe.

Life will continue on because that's what life's made to do. If you are in a bible-teaching church, you will lean on God more than you ever have, knowing you don't control everything but he does. In one of the Bible studies I was in, I remember the minister reading about how a family had a child born with a disease. In the passage, it said something like "Who's to blame for the child being born sick?" The answer was not the fault of the parents, but to prove how big God is, to redeem and love anybody. The answer is, for his glory, he brings people of all abilities to earth.

I forgot how big God is. I think we can all be guilty of forgetting how big God is when nothing challenges us to see Him in a different way. Just like how God wants to get the glory from Miracle's story, he wants the glory in your story, too. If you have a child with a rare disease, or who may be battling something, or you are, know that this story can be an inspiration to others. It is a special assignment to be used by God to play such a big role in an incredible story.

It is moments like this that we realize it is not all about us. It took me a while to get here, but I arrived, and that is what matters. I was in my own way, but I got past it, and you can too.

*Monica Quarles*

*Monica Quarles*

# WHAT CAN FALL DOWN

Life is like a stack of cards. When one card falls, we don't know what cards will go down in the process. So, what can fall down when we are losing grip in one area that impacts another? When I gave birth to my daughter, I had gained the most weight out of all my pregnancies. I was 250 pounds at the time I gave birth to Miracle. During my bout with postpartum depression, I gained another 30 pounds. I was becoming unrecognizable to myself internally and externally.

Before my depression got too bad, I would shop a lot. That was how I coped for as long as it could work. I didn't put us in financial ruin, but I did do a number on our finances. When I wasn't shopping and buying Miracle everything, I was eating, and a lot. I ate food because it was my way of feeling better.

I didn't eat because I was hungry, I ate because it was comforting and I liked the taste of the food I was eating. I ate until I got full and could barely move sometimes. Kind of how people say they eat with their eyes, I was doing a lot of that. Or, I was starving myself and eating nothing. I had huge mood swings that would supercharge or erase my appetite. My body was in a constant state of confusion.

The physical strain on my body for the unwanted pounds was evident. When I would play with Miracle, I would often be sitting down. I didn't do anything that required me to be active. I struggled walking up and down the stairs and would often lose my breath. I knew it was a problem, but I didn't care too much to change it.

I was comfortable with the way I was dealing with my stress. The third way I coped was with traveling. Everywhere I went or wanted to go, I included Miracle. I felt like she needed to see everything and any experience I had, she should have it too. I remember when Miracle was only a few months old and could barely hold her head up, and I was taking her to the movies and the park.

We would go to the museums and the zoo for our day trips. I took her on cruises and all kinds of trips. The Amazon truck was at our house dropping off packages two to three times a week every week. My husband mentioned it to me and said, "Babe. This is getting a little excessive. You're getting two and three packages a week from Amazon." When I was shopping, I wasn't looking at the bottom line, my focus was on Miracle's happiness.

I remember looking at my DoorDash bill and saying, "wow." I loved the app and how convenient it is to eat whatever I wanted. I could pick from any kind of food and even combine items I had a craving for and they would both arrive at my house without me lifting a finger to cook. I didn't choose to go outside for any other reason than for Miracle.

If I was out with my husband, I think he could sense how I was watching the clock and anticipating the moment I would arrive back at home. My relationships with some family and my friends changed dramatically around this time; we no longer shared the same interests. I can't say that I blame them entirely, because I wasn't trying to do anything outside the house or without Miracle. I remember totaling up my food spending, and it was over three thousand dollars!

I knew at that point, I had a problem. I could have used that money to spend time with my children, went on vacation, or did a million and one things other than just eat good food. I tried to do day trips with the family and go to the movies and stuff like that, but oftentimes, I would fall asleep long before the movie finished. I was not present in the way I should have been.

The events I planned were rushed and lacked the quality time aspect, although I was present. I wasn't being a good steward of my finances or my time during this black space of time in my life. I needed to understand that it wasn't about how much time I spent with my children or husband, but the quality of the time I spent with them that mattered even more.

When you are raising a child with special needs, it does take time to care for them. You might feel that twenty-four hours in a day is not enough to meet everyone's needs. But if you only have ten minutes here and there, try and make that time count. Make that time quality spent.

You're not a superwoman, so don't put that kind of pressure on yourself. I can tell you, I hate the analogy that women are superheroes, because it puts unrealistic expectations on women. We get tired like everyone else. We can have bad days, be in our feelings, or make mistakes. Yes, we can do amazing things and surpass people's expectations, but we can also be some regular folks trying to balance time for self, family, marriage, and work. This is enough for us to be special without the added pressure.

You know, another saying I hear a lot that I do love is the phrase, "When you are given lemons, learn how to make lemonade." Yes, there is beauty in the mess. There is a message in the messy parts and uncomfortable experiences. There are all types of cliches and sayings out there that I could add to this book. However, you can't conquer what you don't confront. And I had to confront myself. I had to confront what was really happening in my relationships.

In my marriage, the cards were falling down. He and I had a great relationship, full of fun, love, and intimate affection. After Miracle, a lot of that died between the two of us. Not because of a real reason I could point out, but because we got consumed by Miracle or distracted with other tasks. I wasn't focused on my marriage because I had been so committed to Miracle.

My husband's birthday was coming up, and this was after counseling, so I was in a far better place than before. I was operating on about 10% prior to counseling, therapy, and the things I did to get well. At the time, I was at about 80% of getting back to myself. Things weren't perfect between my husband and I, but we did talk a lot. The touching had died down, and now we had to get the spark back.

I planned a surprise bday and a Valentine's Day getaway for my husband. I choose to take him to his favorite vacation spot - Las Vegas. I booked a four-day trip away from home in hopes we could tap back into the spice we once had. I was ready to get back to being about us. My best friend and long-time friend of 30-plus years, asked me about who was keeping Miracle while we were away on vacation.

I told her plainly, "Oh, she is coming with us." She looked at me with her eyes open a bit too wide, which implied I had said the wrong answer. My other girlfriends who were also there and hearing the conversation had a similar reaction. She said, "I'm gonna keep her for you. And you guys are gonna go have fun and enjoy your marriage." Then the other girls chimed in, "We got you." We're going to watch her."

As she was talking, it was my turn to have wide eyes, and I said, "You want me to leave her?" She replied matter-of-factly, "Yes. She will be fine." I could feel my heart drop to my toes. Miracle and I have been together like white on rice, so it was like a piece of me was going to be left when I was on this trip. I thought of how I would have fun if I weren't sure if Miracle was okay or not.

Before this trip, I had only left Miracle for a few hours tops. When we were having this conversation, we were out at the Symphony for a girls' outing, something I also hadn't done in months. I never went anywhere without her, or expected people to care for her like I do, twenty-four hours in a day. I was like, wait a minute. I have to really trust them with her if I get on this plane. I believed that they would help me if I asked, but had no intentions of testing that theory to this capacity.

It is a bit laughable that I wrote our 20-month-old baby on my ticket and had planned to bring her there sitting on my lap. What was a small baby really going to do in Las Vegas? I wasn't sure, but she was headed for the city of lights before I had talked to my friends. This is one of the pivotal reasons you need a network of committed friends who can be honest with you.

This trip was the best Valentine's Day I had ever had.

We flew out on Vday and just enjoyed each other as we sat, talked, and joked on the plane. The spark was instantly lit, and it was not forced. At the onset of the trip, I felt light and renewed, and the time we shared was precious to my husband and me. It was the most beautiful gift that anyone could give us: the freedom to enjoy our marriage and ourselves. This was the first time in nearly two years that I really focused on my marriage, and it was huge.

Back at home, our other children got to breathe, relax, and enjoy their freedom too. I had been on them over the past two years also with helping me to care for Miracle. I had to have a few meetings to update them about her health and care. I know it wasn't easy for them to hear or see the same articles I was reading. I knew that they were also carrying stress about the future for Miracle, and how we can all be there for her now.

The four day trip we had in Las Vegas, was also a four day trip for our children. I think they needed to be away from us and the high stress environment we had all been living in for the past few years. It was amazing to be in the sun, rekindling our marriage twenty months later. I wanted things to be good between my husband and I, but it meant relinquishing control, trusting our support, and asking for help. I had to get out of my own head so that I could enjoy my life fully even in my circumstances.

I might be going through a difficult time, but I am still a wife, a woman, a mother, and so much more than what I let my life dwindle down to. I had to resurrect myself not just in theory, but also in my actions and commitment to do things differently. February, I feel was really, a pivotal point that I started to reclaim my life and marriage. This was the month that I started to open up with my actions and allow my husband back into all areas of my life, and I retrieved another part of me.

Marriage is about two persons becoming one. When I needed to process my emotions and thoughts, I had pulled away from being joined with my husband. I hadn't realized it, until I was in Vegas and felt the shift. I finally got to give my husband what I knew he wanted too, his friend back. He and I have always been good friends who enjoyed each other. On this trip, we didn't talk a lot about Miracle and the children, but about us. And we just enjoyed each other and spending time together as a kind of rebuilding.

When I got home and saw the condition of my children, my house, and saw that my world was better from my vacation and village, I knew that I had been doing things all wrong. I thought that cards were only meant to decorate the simple parts of our lives, not knowing they are part of the foundation of what we were building too. Words cannot express how grateful I am for my best friend stepping in that day and helping me to do life differently.

I know that this wasn't her first attempt to watch Miracle for me. She has always loved me and my children, and would offer to be there for me. I just wasn't ready to receive the gift of help. Maybe you are struggling too with accepting help from those who are part of your village. Don't run from the hand wanting to help you for too long because other things can be lost in the process.

Can you believe, with two girlfriends who are nurses, and a best friend who has been in my life for nearly two decades, I was blind to the truth that I had help? I think we can see what we want to see and miss what is right in front of us. My village was selected by God, because I know they fit perfectly in my life. I must thank the special people who have been there for me when I needed them.

To my best friend, Alicia, who is my god given sister, ride or die, babysitter and Auntie, God Mom to all my children at any hour of the night, thank you. My neighbor, Idella and Kenny, who would knock on my door to say hi and check on us. For my nurse support, Sarah, Molly and Jordan, Miracle's therapist, and Que her daycare provider and friend. To the Beautiful Butterflies that are always there, providing prayers, meals, and being intentional with me and my family's needs. These people make up my immediate village, who assist me day to day with caring for my family, and I know I can rely on them, no matter the situation.

If you're looking for a sign to know who's in your village, I have a few I recognized. One thing I can see about everyone in my village is that they don't wait for me to ask for help before they offer it. If they see something is happening, they are quick to either meet the need or ask me about it. I have never begged any of them for something; they all either ask me or open the door for me to ask them. These people help out of their own hearts with no ill intentions or expectations of repayment.

Some things you cannot repay, like the time they give to help me and be with my family. It is the things that money cannot buy that make me the most thankful. My support doesn't judge me or criticize my decisions. They are patient with me and keep me open to seeing things another way. There is value in being around people who can support you and not make you feel judged or devalued as they give their help.

When I need some space, they respect that, too. They are not disappointed in me if I don't call or put too much pressure on me to call them. Sometimes the worst question to ask someone is, "Why haven't you called me?" or "What's going on?" These questions can be hard to answer when the answers are not something we want to say just yet.

People who put a lot of pressure on you to call them, but don't call you, remind yourself the phone works both ways. They can call you, and if you ask them not to, it doesn't make you a bad person. I remember when a lot of my supposed friends ghosted me, and the same ones said I disappeared. When I would call, they wouldn't answer. I had to ask myself, "Did I disappear? Or "Did I stop serving a purpose in their life so they dropped me?" It seems like when some people realize the shift in their life because of your absence, that's when they care.

A lot of these friends only wanted to be around me for what I could bring to their world. When I couldn't do that, they didn't want to be around me. It did hurt my heart a lot to see many of my friends and family abandon me when I could have used girl time. I think to cope with the loss of friendship, I redirected that attention to Miracle.

I know my life was tough, and after a while, it became difficult to be around before getting counseling. I don't have a judgment against those who have left, but I had to re-evaluate my relationships and not cry over the things lost, at the expense of looking at what I had. I want to encourage you, too, not to mourn for too long those who are gone, if that means you don't acknowledge who is there.

I know some people pushed away from me because they didn't want to learn about my life and the challenges I face. They knew my situation wasn't normal, and that alone was enough for them to check out. I am sure you felt this too, people who felt like you were too much for them. Try not to let this break your spirit either.

Some of my friends did pursue me, but I wasn't ready to talk. For some of them, I hurt their hearts really badly, and maybe they haven't forgiven me. I am not sure, but I prayed and released the pain I caused in people's lives, like I had to pray to forgive those who did the same to me. I like the part of the Lord's Prayer that tells us to forgive others so that we, too, can be forgiven.

To give you grace, the phone never stops ringing when you have several children, and a child that everyone loves and wants to check up on. It can be hard to call everyone back or to stay organized. Give yourself grace. Allow this shuffling of people to allow you to eliminate friendships you knew were toxic, and put you with the right village you need to move forward.

My life was taking a healthy turn with recognizing my village and dealing with my relationships with my children and husband, but I still had a big problem looming. Shortly after this epic trip to Vegas, I had a health scare that could have taken my life. I'm two hundred and seventy pounds, about 5'5 in height, so it is without question that I am definitely overweight. One eventful day, I wasn't doing anything specific, but I felt a pain in my chest.

I never had one of these before, but when I felt it, I knew what it was. I was having a panic attack that felt like a stroke. I knew after that I had to focus and commit to eating and living better. I didn't just need it, I wanted to create healthier habits so that I can be here for my husband's children, and a huge support to Miracle.

It wasn't hard for me to make a decision to do better. I knew how much my family and village loved, cared for, and needed me. There was no way that I was going to allow a four-day trip to Vegas to be followed by an eternity of separation because I wouldn't get disciplined about food and my health. Thinking about the reality that I could die if I don't get myself together was a reality check I needed to take seriously. Miracle needed me to be here, not just barely hanging on, but healthy and strong.

Our body tells us what we need, and it will scream at us with responses if we are not listening. I had so many signs of the health risk with my weight that I ignored. It is just like God to gently remind us, it's gentle if you are still alive, that he wants to restore all of you. He wanted to bring me back to the image and the heart of who I am, and I had to become a willing participant.

Some things are with God alone. My friends didn't mind my weight, my husband either, but God saw the problem, and he got my attention. My village was there, and yours will be there too, but some journeys you have to do with God yourself. Some things you will have to do for yourself because no one else can do it for you, although they can encourage you to keep going.

It was in a time like this that I realized God never left me. He never stopped loving me and wanting the best for me. And this led me back to him, and I had to rededicate my love to Christ. I had to say in my heart and mind, I will start putting God first and taking the time to care for my connection with God, my physical health, and my emotional health. I am writing this book because my best friend initially inspired me to write it. I really thank God for her and how he uses her in my life to share my testimony to help others.

I didn't even know I was gonna write this book, and I was like, I don't even have anything to say. There's nothing that at present might point to the miracles clearly in my life that the world might agree with me on how I feel. I just have a miraculous story, and a baby who is a miracle. Miracle is a true miracle because we've been living with this rare disease and it has consumed our lives, but I'm grateful because we are making it through it. We have faith she will grow up and live a full and fulfilling life full of laughter and joy.

I press on each day like we all have to, because we want to see the glory that God will get out of our story. I think writing this book has proven me wrong. I have a whole lot to say, and my story is one that should be shared. What I also got from this experience, is writing my story has helped me to reflect on my journey and see how far I have come. Sometimes we have to see it in black and white to recognize our growth journey more clearly.

If we are standing too close to something, we don't get to take in the full view. Miracle is the best thing that could ever have happened to us, and she has matured me and helped me grow in so many different ways. I didn't even realize the depression I was carrying until it was heightened to be detected.

It's a pleasure caring for her, and her lightheartedness, joy, and laughter just helps us along the way. She is a beautiful little girl, and she is not defined by a rare disease. She has a playful personality, she knows what she wants and is not afraid to ask for it. She has sass and she makes a statement when she walks in the room. Her personality is contagious and lovable. She is bold, has so much courage, and she is like our silent giant. Her eyes can say so much. And her smile is infectious.

She is two years old and she still has the G tube. Now, it's been about a year and it is just about certain that she needs a liver. When we came home from Las Vegas, my husband and I faced my health scare but also the findings that Miracle's health and symptoms were getting worse. When we went to her doctor's appointment, her labs and blood work results were not getting any better.

It is hard to see your baby's health declining and hear talk as if she has to get worse before you can take the next step in the process. She needs a liver and the numbers point to that, but some expectations the list might say she needs, could require her condition to worsen. This became a new reminder why praying and keeping hope alive has to be a constant in our lives.

When we are up against seemingly insurmountable odds ,we must keep our faith in God to pull us through it. I knew now, that all the work the Father had me to do on myself, was so that I could become whole again to better protect and advocate for our daughter, Miracle. She needed me to be the best version of myself, not lacking sleep or confidence to better understand everything that was being thrown at us.

Up until this point, I have been seeing things like how they were presented to me. I was hearing the facts, and they were louder in my ear for a season than my prayers. I had to find my voice, confidence, and strength to expand my belief and hope from where it had darkened. Seeing her condition was another wake-up call that the fight wasn't over, but also that I was ready for this battle.

It was saddening to see that her condition had not improved. She itches so bad that she can't sleep at night, which means we don't sleep at night, trying to provide relief. This itching is called "pruritus." A typical night for Miracle consists of sleeping two hours and scratching, moaning, and crying for 6 hours until she falls asleep from exhaustion. She tells us, "Mommy, Daddy, itchy help." It is hard to comfort someone you love in constant pain when you cannot scratch the place that itches. What is bothering her is internal and not external. No cure, just more medication that causes more problems.

It is hard to watch, to listen, to be strong, and not cry with her all the time. She needs us to be strong, and we need God to help us through it. She needs this liver, and I know that even without being a doctor. I asked the doctor, "At what point will she be considered to be on the list?" I would get vague replies that didn't directly answer my question or provide any form of confidence.

Because they couldn't tell me the day, I remember going up to them and advocating for my daughter in their office to get a day. After allowing God to sharpen my voice and confidence, I put it to work in that office. I wasn't timid like I was. I wasn't second-guessing my thoughts; I was confident. I remember saying, "I don't want my daughter to have to be sicker to get on this list. I want her to be on the list, and I need you guys to evaluate her now, please."

And that was how I took my power back and advocated for her in a way that I never had before. Now that I was refreshed, had a new perspective, and time to really think, I could be there for Miracle in this moment. After giving and pouring into myself, I was able to see things much clearly. You know what I'm saying? And you cannot neglect yourself or your children because it will blind you and hold you back from helping those you love.

This day in the office felt great. This was me being the best version of myself and my husband, himself. We stood together in that appointment to advocate for our daughter. We must be authentically ourselves and trust God. This wasn't a death sentence. This was a means for a greater testimony.

I had to lean on the same God who I had trusted to take me through the biopsy and the blood transfusion. He was the same God who took me through the NG tube and the G tube. And now, I need him to be the God of a new liver for my daughter. This requires a level of trust—a commitment to prayer, hope, and discipline. There are things that happen in our lives that will disrupt how we do life. It will make you pray like you never prayed. Fast, like you've never fasted. And believe, like you have never believed before. If you have ever heard that saying to lift your hands as high as you can, then you are asked to reach higher, and you can do it. That proves there is still more in us, even beyond what we thought we had or thought we could give.

I knew, and I still believe, in the presence of God and in His salvation. When we reach this depth, we need a genuine encounter with God to change our circumstances. Not a fairytale, not some good words that make us feel fuzzy, but the real Jesus to step in.

*Monica Quarles*

*Monica Quarles*

# GOD SHOWS UP

God shows up. I learned how to ask for help. And now I can say in this journey that this is where I became empowered, versus being a slave to her rare disease. I realized that I was putting this disease and her diagnosis before a dynamic God, an ever-loving God, a compassionate God, and the only true and all-powerful God. You know, I had to remember who God is, and that was important for my journey ahead.

Although he was showing up all along, I did not see the big and little signs, and I did not put him high. I needed to put him high in this situation with Miracle because I could not carry this burden alone. He said, "Cast your cares off on me because I care about you." "His yoke is easy and his burden is light." So casting my burdens on him became something that I just had to do whenever I felt, you know, I just can't do it anymore.

I learned to call on the name of Jesus more. If I'm tired and exhausted, I would pray, "Lord, she's not sleeping. I'm exhausted. Jesus, help me." I mean, those became very real prayers. It's not about how you sound or what long-winded prayers you can go and throw out there. It is the simple things that he also wants to hear, too.

A simple, "Lord, I know that you can come see about me." I thank God that my circle consist of Christian believers in Christ, no matter our different walks and journeys. Everyone was God sent. God sent them to me and me to them, so that we can help each other carry our burdens. Don't think that because you are going through that, God can't use you. They were praying for me, and I was praying for them. Having people who are praying for you in your circle definitely helps.

I know that for me, as I am going through this situation, I have had to lean on scripture. It was like I was going into the bible, going on a treasure hunt because there are 66 books. There's so much in there to help us grow in God and strengthen our body and spirit. I needed to pull out some nuggets that will help me carry through when I'm not trying to do life in some kind of way. I got to a point where I started to whip out my Bible just because I love God and not ask for nothing.

The best way for me to go to areas in the Bible I need help with now is to Google search topics. Asking for direction on what to read doesn't make you a bad Christian. Reading with expectation is okay, and using the Bible like a medicine book or health guide is also part of its intended use and not just history. I remember praying and then searching on Google, I'm like, "Lord, give me scriptures that can encourage me when I'm down, when I'm fearful. For when I'm alone, when I feel like, you know, I'm not being heard. I know that you hear me."

Then the right scriptures would show up in an article or in the search bar. I sat a time aside for studying and that allowed God to deepen my intention to seek him out in my circumstance. One of my favorite scriptures is, "All things work together for the good of those who love the lord." Like, all things work together. The good, bad, ugly, and the messy. It all works together, you know, for our good. And God has a plan for my life I learned because of Jeremiah 29:11-14, that's my favorite Bible scripture.

> **11** For I know the thoughts that I think toward you, says the LORD, thoughts of peace and not of evil, to give you a future and a hope. **12** Then you will call upon Me and go and pray to Me, and I will listen to you. **13** And you will seek Me and find *Me,* when you search for Me with all your heart. **14** I will be found by you, says the LORD, and I will bring you back from your captivity; I will gather you from all the nations and from all the places where I have driven you, says the LORD, and I will bring you to the place from which I cause you to be carried away captive.

I want to encourage you to know that God has a plan for our lives no matter what it looks like. It is his intention to do you good and not evil, and raise you to his expectations in your life. So there is a future and there is reason for hope. Your child's rare disease doesn't have to be a death sentence. It doesn't have to end your social life, marriage, relationships with friends and your other children. It doesn't have to be the reason why you stop believing in God. The Lord is a strong tower. He can handle all of our problems.

He hears the prayers of the righteous, so never stop praying. I know that the devil tried to keep me in fear. Have you felt that evil and dark place that tries to settle in your heart and make you think you can't do it. When the enemy comes in like a flood, the Bible says God will raise a standard in us! We are told not to be afraid of the terror by day or the terror by night. These are thoughts, medical reports, and anything else that you could hear to bring you to a place of fear. We are to resist the devil, through the power of scripture and trust in God.

I love how the Bible says to pray in spirit and in truth. We have to be truthful about where we are and what we believe. If you don't believe that God is trustworthy or able and willing to help you, share that with God and ask him to increase your faith. You are not the first Christian to pray that prayer and won't be the last.

Even the people walking with God who knew him closely, still needed to be reminded not to be afraid because it's a real emotion. Elijah, sat by the brook after overcoming over 800 false prophets or witches. Jesus prayed in the Garden and meditated so strongly on the prayer that blood came from his pores. It's not a sin that you need help to remember how big God is. If you need a reminder, may this section remind you of how big God is. Remember, we cannot walk in faith, if we remain in a constant state of fear. This is the devil's job. To keep you stagnant in fear.

I remember that I was gripped by fear, and everything I couldn't control brought fear. I was afraid of losing her because I made a mistake or a doctor. I feared the possibility of a surgery going wrong. What if something was done wrong, or her body rejects the surgery? My questions led to the answer being provided by fear and not faith.

Even something simple that most parents don't think twice about with their children made me worried. Most children get banged around and fall down. It is part of being a child. But for Miracle, a fall could bring on a seizure because of how her rare disease impacts her brain.

# God Shows Up

Some people will think you are overreacting because you keep your children in a bubble for their safety. I get it, but what is life if we don't allow them to live it?

Like, that's not living at all if you keep a child from running. If you keep them from enjoying life, and only show it to them. Like I said, I took my baby everywhere, but she didn't necessarily engage with everything. You know? Not being negligent, but just breathing and letting her be a typical one and two-year-old, I had to learn to do. Let her explore and not treat her like a caged bird because of my fear.

I had to put faith around her like I do with the rest of my children. I had to entrust her to God, because only he could truly protect her. I remember when I started to change my actions and allow her more freedom. I remember having a conversation with God, and I said, "Like, okay, God. You got her. Like, help us to remember that you have her, and let's not limit her by her diagnosis." I would say this every time I got scared because I had to trust that she would be fine.

This disease is only a part of Miracle's story; it is not her story. I had to let that light shine, which is his light through her. I just want to thank God because as you read and connect with other believers who are praying for you, you give the Word of God power to change your life. I have to have friends who are able to say, "Come on. Let's pray. Lord, touch this area of Monica's life," and I will do the same for them.

Just having somebody touch and agree with you is very important. My husband and I knew God before, but we have grown spiritually during this process and become better versions of ourselves all around. Yes, it has taken us time to get here, and it is still more after this. Another benefit and constant source of strength for me is listening to gospel or worship music.

For some things in life, words cannot express how you feel. But with the right song and the move of the Spirit (of God), you can be put in the right headspace. There are many times when my moment of prayer turns into singing songs, dancing, and even allowing the music to minister over me, often with tears running down my face. This is one of the most powerful cries you can have. A silent war cry, where someone else is doing the talking, and you are receiving through the spirit. Allow music doesn't lift your spirit, and you gotta watch the songs you play because they carry messages and spirits.

What I love is that Miracle loves to sing. She listens to what I listen to, and it moves her spirit, too! When you are the gatekeeper to your children's spirit, you have to watch what you play around them because it too can encourage their spirit. I watch the words spoken over her life, because God tells us to. You have to watch what you are putting in the heart of your child. Because our words can shape our world, even children's words can impact the world through the power of God!

It's humbling to know and realize how the Father protects us. He is all around us if we open up our hearts to see him. It brings me great joy to know that I am not alone. He didn't just save us from hell, but he also walks with us here on earth if we allow him to. He says he will never leave us nor forsake us.

He saved us from being in the wrong relationship with him. Being in the right relationship with him is important because it removes the limits of what is possible.

## God Shows Up

All things are possible to those who believe. In the right timing, God will do what he said he would do and how he will do it. Our job is to trust that his way is the right and best way. Only his timing is perfect. And I remember thinking about Ecclesiastes three, where the Bible talks about it being a time for everything under the sun. A time for mourning and a time for joy.

There's a time for every season under the sun, and we have to learn how to go through those seasons. But we don't have to go through them alone. I thank God for my best friend who constantly kept me involved with her Women in the Word group on Mondays and invited me to speak at her church. Don't reject invitations to speak about your journey because you are still going through your test.

Remember, this is part of it all, and for where you are now, there is something you can give to someone else. Do you believe that? These invitations also challenge you to remember that life is about more than the test. You have to get in your Bible and read the material, study, to present a Bible study that isn't about what you are going through. It is not the platform to give glory to your challenges or problems, but for you to be used as a beacon of inspiration. This Bible study helped me to keep my eye on Jesus and not my problems.

I think about Job sometimes and how he lost everything. His life was hard; he lost ten children at one time when the roof fell on them. But God! God restored him. He gave Job more than he could ask for or think of. What we think we cannot live through, accept, God can show us how we can do both with his power. I see how we are overcome by the hearing of each other's testimonies. I didn't lose everything, but I did take some losses. And like Job, God is restoring me, too!

Life didn't look how I wanted it to look, and I didn't have the freedom that many people have traditionally had raising Miracle. But, hey, if taking her to the doctor's every 1-2 months is what God empowers us to do to keep her here, I will do it. You know? I didn't have this kind of heart before looking at my situation.

And so you need faith to lean on when you don't see a way forward or the outcome of the next step before it happens. I don't assume that everybody reading this book will be a Christian, but I will hope that choosing a life with God and accepting Jesus as their Lord and Savior will be their choice. I do pray that heaven will be your final destination in light of all the pain you have been through. I know how hard this journey can be, and so I wanted to give you the secret to how I put my life back in order in the midst of the storm.

Life is not perfect, but I wouldn't have gotten this far, without the help of God. I could not have made it out of my depression, without the help of God. I would not be here, without the prayers of my family and friends. I would be alone physically, emotionally, and spiritually if I shut out God. If I stopped trusting God, and putting everything in his hands, my life would be very different. He's looking for people that will love him with their whole heart.

And we don't understand everything. And there's another verse that talks about that. Lean not into your own understanding, but in all your understanding, but in all your ways acknowledge him. Just acknowledge, lord, we're weak, feeble people. We don't even understand everything about this world, and we don't have to.

We just know that you loved us enough to send your Son to die for us in our sins, in our sickness, and our sin you've covered it all. You've paid for it all. And knowing that we're just going through the process, but it's already finished. It's already been accomplished, and we're just going through the journey. Sometimes we neglect to follow the process, but going through the process is how you reach certain destination; all the good stuff is through the journey and what we learned along the way.

God is a healer, not just for sicknesses but for broken hearts too. He cares about your wellbeing and the things you care about. It is not his will to punish you with the disease your child has, but for his glory and your growth to come from it. Nobody has to do anything wrong and sometimes there is no place to point blame. It can be part of your process to show how big God is on earth. Not just for you, but for the world who is watching you and how you respond. You are showing the world, when you have God first, who he is to people who cannot see him.

Just like how he becomes real to you, and is real to me, for those who don't have him in their lives you show them that he is real. Learning that God loves us isn't a punishment, but is critical to having a relationship with God. Having this open door, allows God to reveal himself to you and show you how he is all in all! All powerful.

So when I said that I picked myself off the ground, the Lord picked me up, and I had to raise my hands and say, will you help me to stop feeling sorry for myself. I had to stop feeling sorry for my baby because I forgot that she was a gift. She will be an inspiration to all. Not a calling card of despair but a beacon of light. A light that points to hope. You know? My faith had to rise and maybe yours does too.

I had to take my faith into my doctor's appointments and to the park while I watched her play. I had to make faith the new language that I spoke and the new way I would live. I had to talk positively and think and be hopeful. Sometimes we can get stuck in the mundane things. When we are stuck, we have to be more consistent in protecting our peace, faith, hope, and love. To protect it, ironically, you don't hide it, you share it and make it a bigger part of your life by practicing it every day.

I'm saying, "Lord, not my will, but your will be done" because his will is gonna be done anyway. You know? He's in control. Might as well agree with what he says because he knows best. He can see further than I can, and I know that he loves me and everyone involved.

When I began to trust God again with Miracle, I knew when I went into that doctor's office, something had to change. I can't keep hearing the same thing over and over. My baby's uncomfortable. She needs a new liver.

She's been on medications for months to over a year, and they are not helping her, so it's time. I just started thanking God because I was able to stand in boldness on my position of what our daughter needed. I wasn't alone when I asked for her to be on the list; I had backup! God! The doctor took my request before the doctor's review, and they made an exception for her. Look at God! I am happy to say that we're in that process now, and she was added to the list on May 28th, 2025 for a liver.

Moments like this prove that the hand of God is all over her life, given her favor. I know that my prayers work. I feel like David when he went up against Goliath. The doctors aren't the giants; my fear was to ask, to be

# God Shows Up

accepted or rejected, but the giant was my fear. I had to slay the giant, and I won this battle. I know that this isn't the war. There is still more to do, and I am committed to doing that.

I am praying for Miracle, the donor, and the doctors to all be led by God. I know this is a God thing and we are carrying out his plans. He knows all of our names, skill sets, and what we can handle. When the delays come, I am not discouraged, because I pray through it. I learned a funny saying that people say, "You know, the teacher doesn't talk during testing."

Without a test, there would be no testimony. People can drag their feet or not see how important something is to you until you raise your voice and speak up. You don't have to have all the answers, but be open to making the decision.

I realized that I could not let this rare disease define Miracle, but let Miracle define this rare disease and know that there's hope. She is a beacon of light, and so I decided to start sharing her story. Her being featured in an article was more than I ever thought would happen. She has gotten her fifteen minutes of fame, and we are not even good, and started for the greatest testimony of her life! We are so hopeful for her future and how she will change the world with her story.

Miracle is a living story. She's living out her testimony for all to see what God can do. And so I joined a group, a rare disease group, and I went back and I started looking on the Alagille Syndrome website and decided to start posting there for other families' encouragement. Even though I saw those sad stories before, I didn't look at our situation or what I wanted to share as sad.

I didn't see the stories shared, no matter the outcome, as sad either. I saw the families as being brave. And that's when I said, I wanna be a part of this community and be more involved. So I started talking to people, and definitely doing some things. I wasn't gonna run from it anymore. This website post started a spark that helped to lead to this book because it showed me the need.

I wanted a book that didn't celebrate death, or a rare disease, but the strength of children and parents to be there even when the going gets tough. To remind you that your child is strong. You, as a caregiver, are strong. If you need to hear this again, you're stronger than you think, and God is with you. Whether you are strong in the faith, new to the faith, or not even a believer, you can connect with God to inspire the hope you need to live on.

My prayer for this book is that you leave it having hope. God is the source of my hope, and I believe he is the hope of the world. He's not a God of doom and gloom. He's a God that will hold your hand through your situations and let you know that I Am is here. He will make things right because his ways are not our ways. He can make your life and story beautiful. He can take your tears and allow them to water something great for the world to see. Your tears, you, are precious to him.

He'll give us beauty for our ashes, as the Bible says. So if you are brokenhearted or depressed like I was, he can take the ashes of your life, where the fire burnt them up, crippling your hope, dreams, or aspirations for the future, and give you beauty in exchange. Sadness may last for a night, but joy can come in the morning!

So I would say to any parent to be brave. Be strong. Be intentional.

# God Shows Up

*Monica Quarles*

*Monica Quarles*

# LIVER

So the truth is that Miracle's condition has not improved, but it also hasn't gotten worse other than the itching. It has progressively gotten worse as the medication is not working how it used to. Before, she used to get a good night's rest, but now, she itches so terribly that she has more sleepless nights than anything.

Keeping her nails trimmed has become a greater challenge as she doesn't like it, and the itchiness makes her very uncomfortable and sometimes inconsolable. Now that she's at an age where she can vocalize her pain, she doesn't want our help rubbing her. She wants to do it herself, but the tasks she has are not achievable. To see her so frustrated and in pain pains us both. It's hard to watch. I wouldn't wish this on anybody to have to go through. We try to encourage her and say, "Just a little while longer. Just a little while longer, you're gonna get a new liver.

I'm a social worker by career, but I feel like in the last two years, I've had to become a nurse. I've had to learn more than I've ever wanted to learn about the medical profession. I've had to be a teacher and show others how to care for my daughter.

My journey to learn as much as I know and be able to guide others in her care looks beautiful to me as I play it back in my mind. I didn't have the confidence before when this all started. I didn't think I could handle it all or learn the dos and don'ts. I can do it now with my eyes closed and teach others, but I wasn't always here. I didn't always have the right technique on how to feed her and give her medications to help her not throw up. There were a lot of mistakes.

There was a lot I learned from giving her her medication too fast, which would cause her to throw up and miss that nutrition. I had to learn which medications didn't mix and break them up or give them at different times with or without food. I had to learn the best way to care for our daughter, and you will too. Things will change again, and I will have to remaster what I know now, but my confidence is firm that I will get it. When you have confidence, you are not afraid of the challenges anymore.

Now we're heading towards a liver transplant. There are a lot of moving parts that go into this process, for sure. I am happy and grateful, but also torn because of the implications of Miracle receiving a liver. She is definitely not struggling developmentally. She's talking more than any two-year-old. She's definitely advanced and active, walking and talking beyond her years.

She's met all of her mild developmental milestones, and those were things that doctors didn't think that she would necessarily do because of her eating. Miracle has shown interest now that she goes to daycare for food. She's a social eater, and we will take it. She's learning from her peers, and I love to see how her peers support her. Her childcare facility and nurse are loving and kind to her.

I love that we have a nurse and childcare worker who will spend one on one time with her to allow my husband and I to spend quality time together and get things done. I trust the people in my circle, in my village, to help and want to help us. A group I am also a part of is called the Beautiful Butterflies, and that was another thing that's helped me connect to other women who are going through a metamorphosis and remember to share with others on our journey.

In this group, we participate in giveaways, community projects to feed those less fortunate or give away items people need. It's important to realize that although we are going through changes, the world around us is changing too. Giving to others is a gift in itself, and it feels really good to give to those who can't or won't give you anything in return. It feels like something you truly give away from your heart.

I know we can get busy being a mom, wife, or working our jobs, but making time to give back proves helpful when you need to know who you are. Connecting with people outside your family and village also keeps you aware of how you might be changing and if your feelings are consistent. Sometimes we can put up a face for people and not see it.

Knowing who you are and how you are feeling is good to revisit often. A way I look back on life to check in on my family's growth, is that I often look at pictures. Pictures are worth a thousand words and they can sometimes show what we won't say. I can see the growth in Miracle, my husband, and in all my children–but also in myself.

It's beautiful to see how much we have matured over

the years. The test we have endured has definitely made us all stronger and closer. When I reflect on where we are now, I see how strong Miracle has been. She started off with challenges and she is bravely facing them with all of us here to help.

We are at the start of the process for Miracle getting a liver and the process is undertaken. My husband and I have to lean on each other and our village to get through this. With a disease like this, we know the liver is not the cure all, but it is the next step in our process. Funny, how life throws us all curve balls, so we can never say that we have arrived because there's always more.

Getting on the list was the start, but not the end of this journey. Miracle still will have Alagia Syndrome, but having this liver is going to make her life more bearable. It will help her to win another battle as we continue to fight the war. I never realized how much our liver does in the body. I don't think we really look at what organs do until they don't work, and we have to check with a doctor for a solution.

The liver is what drives toxins out of the body and helps us to absorb nutrients. A functioning liver also helps us fight off diseases, regulates bilirubin, and it does a lot more for digestion and the body. I know that this liver doesn't change everything, but it will increase her chances of eating on her own.

The doctor discussed the possible outcomes of the surgery with us. He said some children don't need the G tube anymore because they wanna eat. Yet, the flip side is some kids don't wanna eat, and they still have to be on the G tube. We won't know how Miracle's story will continue to go forward, but we know that she's strong.

We know that we're not alone. Another real possibility about having a liver transplant is that the body can reject it, and that comes with its own issues. She will have to be on quite a few medications that will help her immune system. The doctor told us that African Americans seem to have overactive immune systems. So, the first thing is to fight anything foreign in the body because our immune system goes into a protective mode for the body. The medication will help with this.

They told my husband and me that she will have to deal with medication management for the rest of her life after the surgery, and if she doesn't get it. This disease is still being studied, and the damage it can cause throughout the body is vast. The liver alone will require her to take medication to help her body manage. They told me that when she was much younger, by the time she turned two, she would need a transplant if her bilirubin numbers didn't improve.

They told me it was a chance that they could correct on their own, and she could make it to 5, 10, or over 18 years old before needing a liver transplant. The timing of her needing one was a question, but it was not really up for debate. Miracle's numbers have not improved but remain stagnant.

Understanding that she may reject the liver, and it puts her at risk for diseases, complications, and even death, are all real scenarios that we have had to talk about. This is where, you know, our faith has to combat our fear. To overcome this realization, we must focus on the greater advantages versus the possibilities of failure. We are holding God's hand through this and facing the risks with hopeful hearts. We know that our God is so much bigger than a liver. He has done great things, and he knows our names; it is only us who don't know how our story ends.

In a process like this, don't worry about the journey; don't dwell too much on the end. Just focus on taking things one day at a time. Another thing that I wanted to do was be my daughter's liver donor because her blood type is B+, and it's very rare. I have a B blood type, and if I were healthy with no issues, I would be a prime candidate. However, because that is not the case, I was removed from the list because of my struggles with weight management and my heart. My husband was also concerned that he would have to take care of both of us, and he didn't think that he could handle that.

Another real fact that we had to realize was that a living donor puts two lives at risk. A living donor could have complications of their own, making a deceased donor the better option. Now, the reality that someone will have to die to give my baby a chance at life chokes me up just thinking about it. It is hard to believe that for Miracle to have the liver she needs, that means a child under the age of seven with a B blood type will have to die.

Once we complete the testing period, we will be added to the list with high priority, and they will search a nationwide database to check for a liver transplant. If the liver is out there, she will likely receive it with her situation. At a time when our family would be celebrating, it is a reality that someone will be grieving their child.

This process reminds me that we all have a birth day and a death day. There is no certain age for when we will die, or we would have no hope for a transplant. This is a circle of life, and the choice for life or death is in the power of God's hand. I think no one likes to talk about death, but it's a reality. I think the fear of Miracle dying was just so heavy on me that I forgot that Miracle has a birth day and a death day, like us all. None of us knows the death date until it has passed, which is why we should enjoy every day we have and be grateful for it.

The truth I found out in life is that no one should want to leave earth with regrets. We want to train up our children in the way that they should go, and also allow them to be children. We should want people to enjoy their youth and not treat it like a plague or annoyance. I think this process has helped me to slow life down in some ways, because as I grow excited for a transplant, we move to a day where another family won't hear their child's voice. See them dance, hear them sing, or live and get older. Another truth we all face, too, is that each day we live is essentially another day that we are dying.

If I could underline anything in this chapter, it would be to cherish the moments you love with those you love, because we all have a birth day and a death day. Talking to my husband about the liver transplant, I cry a lot. I cry for the family in mourning, the life that was lost, and the possibility of saving Miracle's life. It is an overwhelming feeling. I can only thank God for their ability and heart to donate and give us such a precious gift. It's truly a beautiful thing.

Going through this process has made me realize the importance of becoming an organ donor. At the end of my life, I want to donate my organs to a person in need, knowing I did something to bless others who are searching for a miracle, just as we are. To be able to give in your death, beyond grace, what an incredible gift.

This process also shows me that there's beauty in

painful places. It's really a beautiful thing while being a harsh reality. When I was away from my daughter in Vegas those four days, I slept maybe one night. I woke up with her in my heart and imagined any other family to feel like I do about their child, too. I cannot imagine their pain, and their ability to give in this state is a miracle.

When I was in Vegas, I felt some guilt that I was having fun without her. We were glued at the hip, doing everything together. It was hurtful and pulled me out of the moment temporarily to look around and not see her there with me. I didn't let her absence fill my imagination for too long, but the moments it lingered, it was enough pain. It was definitely challenging to still be me in the absence of Miracle. I wanted to feel her love, to nurture her, to love on her, and her not being there was tough.

I am sure she missed me too those four days because it was a first for her also to be away from me. It is a reality that I won't be everywhere she is. Sometimes our children have to be away from us and go through things we don't experience. All we can do is be there or support them how we can. We have to maintain a balance for them and for ourselves; it's healthy.

I had to realize that it was healthy to put my needs first sometimes. I know we can think the lists other people are on is more important than what we have going on. However, we all have value and need to be prioritized on a list. I just thank God for my friends and husband who stepped in at the right time. The Father knew our lives would get busier and needed more of our time to be focused on Miracle. I am glad we took a break when we did to put our marriage and ourselves first.

So don't feel guilty about having a life and being

happy, you know, even though your child is having these different challenges. This is what I have to remind myself for the other family who will have to live on after my daughter's transplant. Her transplant, and with anything in life is not the end, but marks the beginning of something new.

Change is inevitable, because life is on a constant train moving forward no matter the pace. It's healthy for your child to see you enjoying life because they learn joy and contentment through their parents. I don't know if Miracle has reservations for the surgery and process up ahead, but I know if we are confident, she will be also.

If I am hopeful for her future, she will be too. If I prove and point to her resilience, she will do that also. We have to model that self care and that love and balance we want them to have. I didn't want this disease to feel like a death sentence to me, and if that impression were to have rubbed off on her, I wanted to change that. I want her to live her life to the fullest. I don't want to let this diagnosis define her.

There's a risk with everything we do. There is no rule book or guide that will point to every step ahead. We don't know what the process and change will be for us after the surgery. If we will be in the hospital for two weeks or two months. I just wanna encourage any parent who is reading this book to know that it is okay not to have all the answers. It is okay to cry. It is okay to be concerned, even worried or fearful. But–don't allow fear and worry to take over your hopefulness. Don't allow the dark cloud to hover over your joy or memories. Don't allow this disease to take from you, but see it is a part of the story and not the full picture.

This story is not over, and the dates between the dash and how we live life is yet to be determined. What has already been proven, it's a true miracle that we've made it this far and for how far we're gonna go still. In the dark times, allow someone to be the light in your day. Allow them to help you laugh, love, and live. It's okay to let go and trust God and trust your support.

It's not until you let go and realize you can't control the wind that you truly live. And it feels good. So I challenge any person who is reading this book to lean on their support. Those people who say, "Is there anything that I can do to help? Instead of saying no, say yeah."

If we are honest, there are some things that we know we need help with. Sometimes we are silent because we fear rejection. Let me encourage you not to stop asking. Find your village.

Don't stop praying. Don't stop fighting. I know that, when we finally got the okay from the doctors and the team that Miracle was now going to be considered for the transplant list, they explained that it would be a lot of appointments. And they put me in contact with a social worker who would help manage the case. I remember being so excited and saying, "Thank you, Jesus."

The time had finally come, and then fear came to replace the excitement. For about two weeks, after we got the news that she was on the transplant list, I remember having four appointments in one week. I thought my head was going to explode.

The appointments were exhausting, and it was just a reality that this may be our reality for a while until her body recovers from such a massive surgery. I think that's when it really hit me how consuming this process can become. I thought about ensuring that our insurance stayed in place. I got her transplant list card and just made sure all of her appointments were done and on time.

In the midst of all that, I have to keep an eye on Miracle and make sure she is ready and not having any incidents in the morning with vomiting, taking her medication, or eating. Even her going to the bathroom on a schedule and not holding it was a task during those two weeks. Typical toddler stuff was thrown in the mix, and I was being challenged. There is a lot of pressure because anything could pop up and cause delays that we cannot afford. Being late to an appointment was also a no-no.

I remember things slowing down and thinking, *Why is everything slowing down?* The appointments became fewer, and I got an unwanted break. That's when I got the daunting email from her liver doctor that they saw something on her CT scan. So, one of the things that she needed for her evaluation to be placed on the list was to have her blood drawn. After looking at her levels and doing a total body wellness check, there was a problem.

They found a spot on her kidney, at the top of her kidney. They didn't know what it was, and that is the reason for the pause. We were moving so quickly to have her put on the lists, but she cannot bypass addressing her kidney before this surgery. It is uncertain if the spot is a tumor or cancerous, but it will have to be removed before the liver transplant. You cannot have any cancer or tumors present because that will affect the viability of the liver.

Instead of preparing for the life we know she needs, now we have to prepare for a surgery she needs before the transplant. This is an example of the unexpected things that doctors can call and tell you that came up on the image screen. So on one hand, I'm super grateful that they found it, and they can find out what it is. On the other hand, it's like, okay, they're gonna be cutting on my baby and opening her up and working in there.

Here comes the praise report! During the surgery, they found out the mass on her kidney was not cancerous but benign. Even when the surgery caused complications, she got a bacterial infection in her blood and had a respiratory infection. It was a miracle that everything was healed and worked out within three weeks. So, after she was taken off the list because of her kidney, on May 28th, she was added back to the list, and now we wait for the next miracle.

I still believe that she's fearfully and wonderfully made. Things may not be how they should appear, but you know, she needs the surgery to kinda make sure that everything's okay. So it required another level of faith and another season.

So with that in mind, I understand that this will not be a smooth transition. It's hard to prepare for things like that if you can ever prepare because you can think you're ready on one end, and then on the other end, you get some news that takes your breath away. We tried to find out what was on her kidney without surgery, but there is no other way, we were told.

So, our soon-to-be birthday girl had surgery May 7th, just two days before her second birthday. We believe in God in this situation. It's not easy. I would be lying if I said it's easy, but he is the reason we got this far. I am human, please understand, so I need to hear, don't be afraid, like how those in the Bible needed to hear it.

As I write this book, I must believe that He is walking closely with us, His disciples, and I am grateful that He is willing to remind us through hard times that he is always with us. Our minds are so finite, and we don't understand all the movements of God. He's so massive that we cannot even comprehend who he is and his greatness. It's just that we have to take it day by day and be grateful.

During this process, we are not just praying for our family, but also for the doctors. This profession is not easy, and I am sure this process takes a toll on all of us. I am grateful that she has doctors who are taking her condition seriously and looking into everything to ensure the success of this surgery and the transplant.

The teams that are investing their expertise and care to provide for her at every phase have our gratitude. Words cannot share the level of appreciation families have for the doctors and their staff. Meeting the doctors and nurses and seeing how compassionate they are has helped to ease our concerns. Having peace is invaluable in times like these.

Seeing the heart of Christ and knowing that there will be suffering in our days, but also joy, keeps us inspired. Miracle continues to bring us all joy and purpose. One thing the doctor said to me that really still resonates with me to this day is that they said, "Miracle will not remember being sick because she's young. Only you, as the parent, will remember. And so there's something in that for you."

So write your story, journal to release the pain or frustration you might have. Get help, get in a group, lean on your support, because you may be the one who remembers these moments most. I encourage you to write, speak, share, or do whatever you need to do to process this part of your story because it gives healing to the heart. Yes, the ultimate road ahead includes getting her on the liver transplant list, but first, we have to deal with a different piece of the pie, her kidney.

*Monica Quarles*

# CLOSING

In closing, I would like to say that we're not in control. Once we realize that we are not in control, we can truly live. Remember to take life one day at a time. And as you go down this road, or you encourage someone else, remember to say, "I can do this. I'm not alone."

Commit to focus on today because tomorrow is not promised. Yes, there could be a new problem tomorrow, but don't let that make you miss out on today. It's way too much for us to handle to worry about every unknown, so focus on what you know, but always keep hope in a higher regard. I couldn't imagine going through this and not knowing God.

It's my prayer that anyone reading this book doesn't leave it without knowing that God is here for you. I pray that he reveals himself to you. If you were to ask me how I know that he is real or how I know how he feels about us, I would explain it plainly. When I look at my daughter and how much I love her, I know that someone greater than me made me and made her. I know that this strong love I have for her he has an even greater love for both of us.

He is a compassionate God who loves us and can feel our pain. He hears our thoughts and prayers. When we're hurting, he can feel that. When we cry, he keeps every tear. He wants to remind us that we're not alone. When you need encouragement to look into your Bible, to pray in your closet, to use the help of your circle, or find beauty in life outside your world, he can provide it. I'd rather love then die than to have never loved at all.

I know that Miracle is in his hands. And not only is Miracle in his hands, your child, your family, our families, are in his hands. I've learned to realize that this belief doesn't just affect me, but everyone. Miracle brings life and joy to everyone she meets, and I am sure your baby has a similar story to tell.

I thank God for my husband and my children, who are supportive and caring. They hurt just like how I hurt, and my voice isn't the only voice. Miracle has her own voice, and one day, she will be able to say and vocalize how things affected or affects her. There's healing in hearing, and I pray that this book heals everyone who hears it and reads it. I'd be nowhere without God, and I think that Miracle helped me find my way back to him because there's no life without him.

He's our anchor. When we take our eyes off of him, we begin to sink because this life is heavy. I look forward to the relationships that have blossomed, and I pray that I can also be a support for others as well. I thank God for the people who were blessing us just by their presence, their phone calls, their prayers, their meals, and their genuine desire to help us on our journey. The problem that pain has on lives can also be a catalyst for bringing peace, pleasure, and purpose to all things.

We have to learn how to love it all. The good, the bad, the ugly, the indifferent, and the unknown. There's no preparing for anything like what we are going through now. But there is prayer. We can get through it. Knowing that you're not alone is the biggest thing that I would say you should know.

Sometimes our lives need modifications, and those modifications are beautiful. I've gotten to spend so much time with Miracle and gotten to know her fully. Her personality is dynamic, and watching her grow over these two years has blessed me. I've got to watch my husband grow as a father, as a husband, and as a hard worker. I've got to see myself grow and prioritize self-care when I've lost myself in my assignments and other duties as a mother, wife, and social worker.

I have a responsibility to myself. You can only pour out when you're full or have something to give. You can't give anything when you're empty. So I want to give a good version of myself to my family, to my children, to my daughter. She's a true miracle because she's helped me live again. And there were some dead things in my life that needed to be resurrected through this situation, through this diagnosis.

I can say that I have seen our children step up and be a help to us, too. Seeing them mature and work through fights on their own has not gone unnoticed. I appreciate how they have given me the time to spend with Miracle and to work with her, and not resent me for it. I thank them for their patience and growth over the past two years.

Yes, there is still more for us all to learn, grow through, and do. I will admit that I have had to learn more about our bodies and how we have to take care of them and cherish them since Miracle's diagnosis. Life is a beautiful gift. It is my prayer that none of us will waste it on thinking about death, because death is just a new beginning. I just wanted to share my journey because I believe we all need a community and a safe place to talk and share miracle stories, encouraging others to share their own.

"As I was getting this book to the printer, I got a message that said the story is not over. I got a call that said Miracle got the liver we had been waiting for! I know this is the next step in the process, but I am excited to be here now. God is still showing up!"

Until next time.

Miracle's journey continues.

**SCAN ME**

**Call or Text:**
**770-240-0089 Press Extension 1**
**Web: KLEpub.com**
**Email Services@klepub.com**

It's time to start and finish   **YOUR  Story!**

KLE Publishing specializes in helping people become authors. In as little as 15 to 90 days, we can help you develop your books and e-books and publish to 39,000 outlets! We also offer audiobook services.

**Write, Edit, Format, Publish**
We can help from
**Start to Finish.**

# Explore and learn more about published authors affiliated with KLE.

# KLEPub.com

www.ingramcontent.com/pod-product-compliance
Lightning Source LLC
Chambersburg PA
CBHW061759070526
44586CB00023B/2637